Maria Simpson

Roseville Seminary

A temperance Story

Maria Simpson

Roseville Seminary
A temperance Story

ISBN/EAN: 9783337077150

Printed in Europe, USA, Canada, Australia, Japan

Cover: Foto ©ninafisch / pixelio.de

More available books at **www.hansebooks.com**

ROSEVILLE SEMINARY;

A TEMPERANCE STORY.

BY
MARIA SIMPSON.

Toronto:
HUNTER, ROSE AND COMPANY.
MDCCCLXXVIII.

TO

Our Lord Jesus Christ,

THE GREAT CAPTAIN OF THE TEMPERANCE ARMY

THROUGHOUT THE WORLD,

THIS LITTLE BOOK IS REVERENTLY

Dedicated

BY

THE AUTHOR.

CONTENTS.

	PAGE
CHAPTER I.	
HIRAM MCROSS	9
CHAPTER II.	
"DISTILLED DAMNATION"	22
CHAPTER III.	
YOUNG MCROSS IN TROUBLE	29
CHAPTER IV.	
"SUNDAY AT THE SEMINARY"	43
CHAPTER V.	
"TEMPERANCE ON THE BRAIN"	56
CHAPTER VI.	
THE HOLIDAYS	65
CHAPTER VII.	
"TEMPERANCE FOREVER"	73
CHAPTER VIII.	
"FATHER AND SON"	85

CONTENTS.

CHAPTER IX.
"Hattie Mays" 99

CHAPTER X.
"Giant Despair" 118

CHAPTER XI.
"The Rumseller's Lament" 132

CHAPTER XII.
The True Church 139

CHAPTER XIII.
Ronald McFarlane 154

CHAPTER XIV.
The Pupil Teacher 172

CHAPTER XV.
Mr. Grant's Return to Roseville 189

CHAPTER XVI.
"That Blessed Boy" 194

CHAPTER XVII.
Confiscated Liquor 204

CHAPTER XVIII.
The Temperance Banner 220

ROSEVILLE SEMINARY.

CHAPTER I.

HIRAM M'ROSS.

"WELL, Tom, you see I have come to this Seminary, as you so strongly recommended. Why did Mr. Grant establish it in this lonely place?"

"From regard to our morals, Thorne," replied his comrade, in a mocking tone. "We are just a mile from Roseville, and are not allowed to go even to that miserable little village, except on Sundays, when Mr. Grant marches us all to the Congregational Church. He is religious, but very cold and reserved; while his assistant is one of the most snarling, hateful men you ever came across."

"Not a very favourable account of my future teachers," laughed George Thorne.

"You will wish to know the names of the scholars. That's Archie Campbell, running between those snow-forts. He is just sixteen, and quite popular in the Seminary, but *I* don't like him, for he's a saint."

"A Christian, I suppose you mean, Tom. My mother is one, but *I* am not; and so much the worse for me. Who is that lad over there?"

"Hiram McRoss. He has done nothing but go to school all his life, though he has only been with us for two years."

" How old is he ? "

" Nearly twenty. Hiram has a fearfully bad temper, and yet makes out he is a Christian."

" Poor fellow! " exclaimed the sympathizing Thorne. " It must require a good deal of grace to subdue a constitutionally hot temper. How long has he been a Christian ? "

" Only about a year, and, to confess the truth, he has improved greatly since then. If Mr. Slow were not so snarly, Hiram would have a better chance."

In the evening, the new-comer formed acquaintances with several of the scholars. At nine o'clock they were summoned to prayers; then the Principal sent them off to bed, Thorne being permitted to room with his friend.

" Isn't this a very gloomy place, Tom ? "

" Of course it is. That's why I wanted you here. Misery likes company."

George laughed. Then his thoughts going on a different tack, he inquired, " Is not Ivon a dear little fellow ? "

" Yes, he is, Thorne. That ten-year-old child has set his heart on being a minister. Now, my old chum, what do you think of the Principal ? "

" Indeed, Tom, I feel a little afraid of him ; for I never got on well with my teachers, and it will doubtless be the same here. Of course I am eighteen; but, in case of trouble, what chance would you and I both together have against that monstrous Yankee ?"

"None at all," said Tom emphatically, "and believe me, George, that, in regard to Mr. Grant, 'discretion is indeed the better part of valour.'"

As they were talking in a similar manner, Mr. Grant's step was heard in the hall. He suddenly opened the door of their room, and said sternly, "I expected this, Tom. You have not made the slightest preparation for bed. Perhaps you intend to sit up all night, and are welcome to do so, but it will be in the dark." So saying, he took their lamp away and closed the door.

"Oh, what a hateful man!" exclaimed George Thorne, when the master was well out of hearing; "I wanted to unpack some things."

"It's just like Mr. Grant—a fair specimen of what he always is. There's not a scholar that cares a snap for him, except Hiram McRoss. But come, Thorne, we shall have to go to bed in the dark."

When George entered the schoolroom on the following morning, he found nearly all the lads present. The assistant's nephew, Giovanni, a boy of fourteen, immediately began to unfold a large roll.

"What is it?" inquired the new student.

"The Temperance Pledge," replied the boy. "Please put your name down, Thorne. Mr. Grant won't sign, neither will Hiram McRoss; but all the other scholars have and the assistant also. Follow their good example."

"I don't think I'll do it," laughed George.

"You might just as well take it first as last," observed

Tom, impatiently. " Giovanni won't give you a moment's peace till you do."

Hiram McRoss with other lads drew near them.

" So all the names are down except those two," remarked Thorne. " Is the Principal fond of his glass ? "

The boys laughed, save McRoss, who turned angrily toward the new-comer.

" Excuse me, Hiram," said George, " I had no idea that you were so touchy about the head-master's reputation."

" A hundred times more than he is about his own," returned Giovanni. " Mr. Grant was never given to drinking—he will not take a drop of liquor; but, unfortunately, he has a strong aversion to a pledge."

" He is so stiff and cold," observed Shuter, " that none of us like him, except Hiram McRoss."

" Perhaps the master is partial to *him*," suggested Thorne.

" *Very*," sarcastically returned Tom. " He is harder on Hiram than on the rest of us. Happily, flogging is never practised here, or——"

McRoss laughed. " I should stand a good chance, you mean, Tom ? I'm perfectly aware that I should."

" Oh, I'm so sorry that I came," said George.

" Now, don't parley any longer; sign the pledge at once," urged Giovanni.

" What makes you attack him so soon ? " asked Ivon.

" The demons reminded me of it."

Thorne started and shivered. In his childish days he had been in mortal terror of ghosts, and was not strong-minded still. "I don't know what you mean," he said at length.

"Why Thorne," Giovanni replied, "the Demons, you know, of Demon-land and Destruction." So saying, he ran out of the room, but soon returned with a large lithograph—a temperance lecture in itself. Shuter held it, while Giovanni took his uncle's pointer and explained it all to George, who asked, "Do you keep that picture in your room?"

"Yes; and those demons are the first things my eyes rest upon in the morning."

"I should dream about them if I slept with you," remarked George, with a shiver.

"I often do," answered Giovanni, coolly. "This morning uncle brought me a light, and my eyes rested on the demons as usual; but I was sleepy and dozed off again. Suddenly they grew to life-size and danced about my room with horrible grimaces. One came and leaned over me, saying, 'If *you* don't get George Thorne, *we will!* I felt his fiery breath as he grinned in my face, and tried to push the hideous creature off, so that I wakened with a start."

At the risk of being called a coward, Thorne immediately promised to take the Pledge.

"I'm glad of it," replied Tom, "you are a generous, warm-hearted fellow, George; just such an one as the demons delight to entrap."

Giovanni put a pen into his comrade's hands, saying solemnly, "*By the help of God,* you know, Thorne."

"Yes," replied George, and he signed his name.

"Thank-you," said Giovanni, earnestly; and he carried the rolls back to his room.

Mr. Slow's patience was tried more than usual by the morning's school-work, so, at the dinner table, he snarled forth, "I have often counselled my superior to commence corporal punishment in the Seminary. I am sure, Hiram, that a horse-whipping would be the best thing you could have."

"You had better horse-whip me, Mr. Slow;" hotly returned the lad, "I'll warrant, *you* would get the worst of it!"

Mr. Grant sternly interposed, in behalf of his gray-haired assistant. "I'll take good care to prevent *that*, young McRoss. Should corporal punishment be introduced here, and you need flogging, I will take you in hand, myself."

"Thank-you, sir," replied Hiram, quietly.

The boys laughed, save Thorne; and Mr. Slow observed, "you seem surprised, George, but the Principal would just as soon flog lads as old as Tom, yourself, or Hiram McRoss, as the youngest boy in school. He is very eccentric!"

"Not half so eccentric as you are yourself," said Mr. Grant, laughing. While Thorne looked across the table at the monstrous Yankee with a feeling of dread and disgust, the latter resumed. "How did you vex my assistant, young McRoss?"

Hiram coloured, but he replied candidly. "Mr. Slow told me to work a long problem in cube root. I said I could not do it. He would not believe that, and sent me to the black-board. I was cross and stood there for half-an-hour making figures, but not trying to do the work right. Of course the answer was wrong, as I knew it must be, for I made lots of mistakes without taking the trouble to correct one of them."

"You may well look ashamed of yourself," said Mr. Grant, sternly.

"That's what *I* think," laughed the assistant. "I suspected that he was not trying very hard, but could not be sure."

"What will you say, young McRoss, if I make you stay in for two hours this afternoon?" asked Mr. Grant.

"Say that I am justly punished, sir."

"What surprises you, Thorne?" asked Mr. Slow.

"I was told that Hiram had a very hot temper, sir," thoughtlessly answered the perplexed George.

"And so he *has*," snapped the assistant; "you will soon see for yourself, but he does not show it much to the head-teacher. Hiram is also proud and independent to a fault, so much so that his name ought to be 'Touch-me-not.' Just one of you put your hand ever so gently on his shoulder and it is sure to be pushed off in a hurry. Mind you, though, he hasn't the slightest objection to the hands of our worthy Principal!"

The lads grinned; and Thorne, seeing that Hiram looked much confused, changed the subject by saying, "I do hope the day will keep fine. Your favourite game of Soldiers' I never saw played before, and am all eagerness to join in. But I must have Hiram McRoss for my captain, and not James Bell."

"You forget that I have to stay in, Thorne. You may be captain in my place; and, *mind you uphold the honour of the 'Stars and Stripes.'*"

Seeing Thorne's look of surprise, Shuter volunteered a word of explanation. "Hiram is of Scotch parentage, George; but, in our play he always fights under the American flag. I'm sure you can guess the reason:" and he laughed.

"Will you feel disappointed at being kept in," asked George.

"I don't mind the punishment," replied Hiram gravely, "but——"

"But what?" grunted Mr. Slow. "Finish what you were going to say, if you are not ashamed of it."

Hiram's face reddened, as he abruptly added, "but—I am *sorry* that I vexed Mr. Grant."

The dark eyes of the Principal rested on "young McRoss" so lovingly, that the gloom melted from his face at once, and the derisive laugh of the assistant fell unheeded on his ear.

The lads were soon dismissed to the play-ground. "I would have tried evasion and not criminated myself as you did;" remarked George to Hiram, "then, who would have known that I was at all to blame?"

"*God* would!" replied Hiram McRoss.

Thorne was considerably taken aback; he answered very gravely, "You're *right* and I'm altogether *wrong*."

Tom hastily drew George away.

When lessons were over for the day, and the teachers had withdrawn from the school-room, Shuter exclaimed, "Oh, how provoking! I did long for a good play; and, just look, it is a real tempest out-doors."

"We shall have to be content, here."

"It will be *dis*content with me, Thorne. Now, there's Giovanni, studying his Temperance books as usual. Let the wind howl ever so loudly, it never troubles *him*."

"Has he imbued *you* with his queer notions?"

Shuter laughed. "He has imbued us all, more or less; though Hiram stands out against him still. The first thing that Giovanni said to him, on his arrival here, was, 'Please McRoss take the Temperance Pledge.' But he refused, and has never done it."

"And never will, probably," remarked Thorne. Then pulling Shuter by the arm, he walked over to Giovanni and playfully snatched the book out of his hand. However, he soon gave it back saying, "Text-book of Temperance! What a dull thing!"

"It's deeply interesting," returned the owner.

Thorne, laughingly remarked, "Now, Giovanni, I hear that you pestered Hiram nearly two years ago to take the Pledge. Doubtless, you have long since given him up in despair?"

"Given him up!" exclaimed Giovanni, with a look of amazement, "oh, never!"

"When did you last speak to him of Temperance?"

"This morning," returned Giovanni, gravely.

Thorne looked merrily at his companion.

"How long did *you* stand out against him, Shuter?"

"Only three days; and I'm not sorry."

"Neither am I, if this is the way he plagues us."

"Is it for *his* good or our's, Thorne?"

"I suppose it's for our's," answered George. "What makes you so strongly in favour of Temperance?" he added, addressing Giovanni.

"I've had reason enough; don't ask me, please," and a look of pain came over the boy's pale face.

Thorne turned hastily away, and went up to the desk where Hiram was studying. Forgetting the character of his companion, he put his arm around his shoulders.

"Keep your hands off me!" said McRoss, angrily, giving the friendly arm a rough shove.

"I'll try to remember the next time," answered Thorne, mildly.

"I thought you did it to tease me, but, you must go away, George, or *you* will get into trouble. I am kept in."

The new scholar hastily retreated, and rejoined his comrades in another part of the room. At last, Archie said, pityingly, "Hiram has doubtless been puzzling over that problem all this time, and we are not allowed to go near him. He has still twenty minutes to stay in. How tired he must be! Hush!—here comes the head-master! He cannot walk over to Roseville, as usual, for it is so very stormy."

George saw that Hiram was not aware of the Principal's approach, until a hand was laid on his curly, black hair. *That* hand was not pushed off; but Hiram looked up to Mr. Grant with a bright smile.

"It's all right, now," said Archie, as the master seated himself beside his favourite and began to help him through the difficulty.

Thorne nudged his comrade's arm. "Did you ever see such a different expression on a boy's face?" he asked.

"You mean," replied Campbell, "that Hiram was troubled and puzzled a few minutes ago, while now he is so happy."

"No, but that's quite true. *I* meant that Hiram is such a manly-looking boy, far more so than the rest of us —than Bell, even, who is two years older. But just glance at him, *now*, and tell me if you ever saw a boy of his age look so much like a child?"

"I never did;" replied Archie Campbell, smiling. "But, you must remember, Thorne," he added gravely, "that there is no other person living who has such influence over Hiram as the Principal. To *him*, McRoss is a child; for, he often calls him so. And, as for Hiram, if he were ten years old instead of twenty, he could not appreciate Mr. Grant's petting more than he does now. Indeed, I greatly doubt, if there is a child living, who enjoys his parents' caresses as much as Hiram does those of Mr. Grant!"

"He is a big baby," said George Thorne, with a good-natured laugh.

Soon the tea-bell rang, and the scholars hastened to obey the summons. The Principal put his arm around Hiram's shoulders and they went in together.

"You like Mr. Grant to pet you, McRoss," remarked George.

"Indeed he does," said the assistant, "and my superior is very fond of him." He then added, addressing the Principal, "is there anything, on earth, that you care about besides Hiram?"

"Yes," replied Mr. Grant, with a sudden fire in his dark eyes, "*my country!*"

"I might have known that," grunted the assistant, "for that lovely 'Star-spangled Banner' waves over your head, every night; your rooms are all decorated with framed copies of the 'Declaration of Independence,' pictures of George Washington, and the battles of Princeton, Trenton, etc. I dislike them all; but the one that is the *most* odious to me is the 'Surrender of Cornwallis.'"

"*I* like it," replied Mr. Grant, with a smile; "it speaks to me of victories dearly bought, of independence gloriously achieved; but to you, *an Englishman*, it is a symbol of ——" the Principal stopped abruptly.

"Do go on," sneered Mr. Slow.

"It is quite unnecessary, sir," was the calm reply, "you may finish it as you please."

The assistant mockingly remarked, "you love your country, Mr. Grant."

"*Yes*," said that gentleman, his face glowing, "and I would willingly give my heart's blood in her defence."

"That's more than I would do for *mine*," snarled Mr. Slow. "Of course, England is a fine old spot; but, I should be very sorry to have to die for her! There is no wonder that the Principal deeply regrets his youthful mistake of settling in Canada and investing his property with us. However, he consoles himself by taking a trip to the ' Other Side ' every year."

" You are not much of a patriot, sir," laughed Shuter.

" No," snapped Mr. Slow ; then, to effect a diversion, he suddenly began to attack his nephew by describing the forces of liquordom—how they controlled men, money, and parliamentary votes—of the enormous amount of capital employed in the traffic, etc. He then asked,

" How *can* you expect that the Prohibitionists will ever overcome ? "

Giovanni's Temperance literature came to his aid, and he earnestly replied, " But uncle, *God* is on our side ! How many did you count *Him* for ? "

" You always give such a queer turn to things, my nephew ; I never thought of Him at all."

" Well, sir; but you think of Him *now.* Have those who love the Cause of Temperance any reason to despair ? "

" My nephew—you are determined to corner me. Why —why—of course, with *God* on your side, the success of the Temperance Cause is merely a question of time ! "

CHAPTER II.

"DISTILLED DAMNATION."

N the evening, the assistant came into the school-room, and was talking with Ivon when Thorne joined them, and inquired, "why did *you* sign the pledge, Mr. Slow?"

"It's a long story. Giovanni hates the sight or smell of liquor; he never took a drop in his life."

"And *much* he's the better for it!" exclaimed Thorne. "He's slender, pale, and consumptive-looking."

"Yes;" snarled the assistant; "but if you had been half-starved and half-clothed for the first ten years of your life, perchance, Mr. George, you might be slender, pale, and consumptive, too!"

"Oh, Mr. Slow, was Giovanni like that?"

"Yes; and what was worse, he saw his mother die a lingering death of grief and starvation together. Her husband, the miserable wretch, just killed her by inches."

"Poor boy: I am very sorry for him."

"And so am I, Thorne; for he will never be a strong man; *never!*"

"What became of his father, sir?"

"Oh, he *drank*. The less said about him the better. Mind that you never mention his name to Giovanni. I have taken the best care I could of my poor sister's only child; came out from the old country to do so, in fact."

"He is thriving under your care, sir."

"Yes, Ivon, I'm glad of it. Well, when on the road here, about three and a half years ago, there was a person on the stage with us, who was evidently a drinking character. My nephew, after much coaxing, induced him to sign the Pledge. Some days after our arrival, Giovanni took ill of scarlet fever. I am sure he got it from that ragamuffin on the stage. No sooner was he better, than Mr. Grant and myself were both down with it. Giovanni would not take a drop of liquor. When the doctor poured out a glass of wine for him, he threw it in that gentleman's face. The physician was angry enough to have shaken him; but he dared not do it. I gladly took all the liquor that was ordered for me; and, when better, placed the wine and brandy that remained, in a dark closet. Now, you will think me superstitious, Thorne, but I firmly believe in ghosts——"

"Oh, don't tell me a ghost-story!" interrupted Thorne, with a scared look.

"I'll do nothing of the kind. For years I had been in the habit of taking a little brandy, or whiskey and water the last thing at night; so of course I did, after getting well of the fever. Once, when bed-time came, I went for a dram as usual. To my horror, instead of seeing 'Fine Old Cognac' on the brandy-bottle, there were the words 'Distilled Damnation.' That Giovanni had put it there, but in my sudden fright I attributed it to the work of some fiend, who was likely concealed in the dark closet. So I slammed the door to in a hurry, and whacked the bottle against it. My fanatical nephew gave me no peace after that, until I signed the Pledge."

"I'm very glad that you did, sir;" said Ivon. "Now, persuade the Principal to sign also!"

"I won't," snarled Mr. Slow. "Giovanni, even, cannot get *him*. The master thinks me far below him—he is cold and reserved, and evidently does not regard *me* as an English gentleman!"

McRoss had come up in time to hear the last words; so he replied, "I'm sure, sir, that if you would *behave* as a gentleman, you would be treated as one. No one could possibly be more just than Mr. Grant!"

"You take his part through everything," laughed Ivon, "though he has punished you far more than the rest of us."

"That was because I richly deserved it."

"I cordially agree with you *there;*" said the snappish Mr. Slow. Then, as a number of the lads drew near, he joyfully embraced the opportunity of taunting McRoss about his religion, sarcastically remarking, "If all Christians are like Hiram, then I never wish to be one!"

"That's a shame!" exclaimed Aleck Shuter, "*I* am a Christian, too, and Mr. Slow often attacks me on that score; but *I'm* not disheartened by him as Hiram is. Religion *has* improved him and no mistake—(don't go away McRoss, please); for, when he first came here, Thorne, he was the most passionate, cross, hateful fellow you ever saw. He beat every boy in the school, and actually thrashed the assistant teacher once—for which *I* wasn't sorry!"

"You detestable scamp!" exclaimed the angry Mr. Slow. "It's all quite true what you say. That bad boy was guilty of everything almost, save insubordination to Mr. Grant. The eccentric Principal took a strong liking to him from the first."

"McRoss amply returned his love," laughed Shuter, "and, since becoming a Christian, he has managed to keep his hands off us; though some of the lads and the snappish assistant have often provoked him fearfully. I am sure that he tries to do right, not so much to please Mr. Grant, as to honour his Lord and Master."

"I have never been anything but a disgrace to Him!" returned Hiram bitterly, as he moved away from the group.

Mr. Slow rejoined his superior in the large library-parlour, and gleefully remarked, "I've just been telling the lads that 'if all Christians are like Hiram, I never wish to be one!'"

"You surely did not say such a cruel thing before young McRoss!"

"*Yes.* He hung down his head and looked so sad and ashamed."

"You will be sorry for that, *one day;*" said Mr. Grant, sternly. "Supposing, Mr. Slow, that young McRoss and yourself both died to-night, I would ten thousand times rather be in *his* place than in *yours!*"

B

"So would I!" snarled the assistant. "You take to yourself the credit of his conversion—doubtless you do!"

"Credit! There is nothing of the kind about anyone's conversion. The glory belongs to God alone. Those we bring to the Saviour are our spiritual children; *ours*, not only in time, but through the endless ages of eternity!"

"So *you* are Hiram's father!" observed Mr. Slow, in a mocking tone.

"*Yes;*" replied Mr. Grant, his eyes shining with joy, "and I am very thankful for it."

"You take precious good care of your *son*," sneered Mr. Slow. "Those scientific books take up far too much time (ay, you may well colour!); upon my word you are a model father! Turn over a new leaf!"

Meanwhile the lads were in the school-room, talking earnestly enough.

"Hiram, *why* won't you take the Pledge?"

"What a torment you are, Giovanni! Because I *like* liquor. We always have cider or beer on the dinner-table at home; and I can help myself to Aunt's elder and currant wines, whenever I choose. Every night we have a glass of rum and water, sweetened with molasses; which is nicer than the rest. Father has followed the sea from youth, with the exception of a year or so. Sailor-like, he is fond of his grog; and, since becoming a captain (eight years ago), drinks more of it than ever. I must take after him, for I am fond of it, too. Whatever are you crying for, Giovanni?"

"Poor Hiram! Poor Hiram!" sobbed the boy.

McRoss answered gravely, " I don't think that I am in much danger of becoming a drunkard; but if it were so, you need not cry over me, for I am not worth it."

" You said you would sign when Mr. Grant did."

" Yes—he is not likely to do it."

Giovanni brushed away his tears and left the room. In a moment or two more, he was standing before the Principal, saying earnestly, " Sir, you refused to take the Pledge, some time ago, although you knew Hiram would sign as sure as ever you did. He is in danger, for liquor is on the table every day at home, and during vacation, he has to endure constant enticement. Beside that, he is fond of grog !"

"*Fond of grog!*" echoed Mr. Grant, aghast at the thought.

" Yes; he said so. What else could you expect from the son of a drinking sea-captain ?" The Principal looked bewildered. " I thought that he was brought up on a farm ! "

" So he was, sir; and they have lots of liquor there. He is in great danger; and *you*, the only one on earth that can save him, *won't* do it. Poor Hiram ! May God help him ! If he died a drunkard, ou *your* head will be the blood of your beloved young McRoss !"

The Principal rose and immediately turned Giovanni out of the room. However, the next morning he announced his intention of signing the Pledge, and asked his favourite to do so with him.

Hiram's cheeks flushed. " Don't take it on *my* account,

sir. I would have signed it long ago, had I thought *you* wished it."

"My dear boy," answered the Principal, "I prefer to take the Pledge with you. It will not injure either of us."

"Ho! Ho!" laughed the assistant, "You might both just as well have signed two years ago, instead of standing out against it for so long and *giving in* at last!"

"Uncle! Uncle!" exclaimed Giovanni, "You will set them against it for good. Do be quiet!"

"I have come to the conclusion that it is *right* to take the Pledge," said the Principal, gravely, "and I trust that all the sneers in the world would not hinder me from doing my duty."

"'Tis a pity that you did not see it in that light before!" sarcastically returned Mr. Slow.

Shuter laughed. "It is from *pure benevolence* that the Principal employs you, sir; I am certain of that, and so are we all!"

"Mind your own business, you insulting lad," growled the assistant, who knew that it was impossible for his superior to deny Shuter's assertion.

A few moments more, and Mr. Grant and Hiram both signed the Pledge, greatly to Giovanni's delight.

CHAPTER III.

YOUNG M'ROSS IN TROUBLE.

THE studies proceeded as usual that day until after recess, when the assistant marched over to his superior, and growled, "It is too bad; I explained a difficult problem in Algebra, yesterday; and yet, only two lads got it right this morning. Come and see for yourself!"

The Principal complied, and inquired: "Whose is that work on the blackboard?"

"It is Archie's," said Mr. Slow.

"Show the lads how you did it, Campbell."

"Yes, sir;" and Archie obeyed the Principal.

"That was first-rate," remarked the assistant.

"I would like to see *you* go over those explanations, young McRoss," said Mr. Grant, gravely.

"I couldn't," replied Hiram.

"That is just what I thought," continued the Principal. "You were not paying the least attention; for I watched you closely."

"Pity that you weren't better employed," crossly returned Hiram.

Mr. Grant was surprised, for the lad had rarely spoken disrespectfully to *him*. He rubbed off Archie's work, and said sternly, "you shall have the pleasure of doing this long problem from the beginning, young McRoss. This is Saturday, and if you wish to be free in the afternoon, I advise you to redeem your character."

"I can't do that problem."

"You can *try*."

"*I won't ;*" and Hiram threw down his chalk on the floor in a passion, and went off to his seat.

"What a delightful specimen of human nature is that same Hiram McRoss," observed Mr. Slow.

The usual lessons proceeded until twelve o'clock, when the school was closed till Monday. As soon as dinner was over, and the two teachers were alone, the assistant observed: "You're in a 'nice fix,' sir. Being an American gentleman of ample means, and merely teaching for pleasure, you have always summarily expelled those lads who were guilty of insubordination. Hiram *knew* that; but he has set your authority at defiance, thinking that you will not expel *him*."

"I shall horse-whip him instead."

"Horse-whip him?" exclaimed the amazed Mr. Slow. "Why, Hiram is nearly twenty years old, and has often boasted that he never was flogged in his life. That disgraceful punishment was never practised here, and for you to inflict it on your favourite! He will go into a fearful passion before he gets the first stroke."

"I fully expect it."

"As sure as ever you do, he will pack up his things, and leave by stage to-morrow."

"I'm afraid so," said Mr. Grant, sadly, "but there is no help for it. I cannot expel him; for there is no one on earth that I love so dearly; therefore, the only alternative is to flog him, or I should be unjust to the school, and *very* unjust to young McRoss."

"Be prepared for his violent resistance."

"Certainly—I quite expect it."

"Now, sir, please listen. Don't, pray don't, flog him hard enough to make him cry. If you manage to draw a tear out of that proud, independent lad, he will *never* like you again."

Mr. Grant smiled. "You are mistaken, Mr. Slow. He does not seem to mind what *you* say at all; but it is almost impossible for *me* to scold him without making him cry."

"You astonish me, sir. That *proud* Hiram McRoss; are you sure you are correct?"

"I could not well be mistaken, my assistant, for I have often wiped the tears off his cheeks."

Mr. Slow laughed. "Indeed, I congratulate you on your influence, Mr. Grant; I am glad you can make him cry, for it's what no other living creature can do! I have seen enough of Hiram McRoss to know that. So *that's* why you always scold him in private, is it?"

"Certainly; it would hurt his feelings dreadfully if his companions should see his tears."

"Well, you *have* astonished me. As for his leaving the Seminary, I am convinced that there is not the slightest danger of it, and it is quite safe for you to flog him as hard as you choose!"

"I *hope* so," said the Principal, doubtfully. "He has

just come in, so I will go to him now." Which he did, locking the school-room door after him. Hiram was standing just below the platform. Mr. Grant unlocked a drawer in his desk, and took out the formidable instrument of punishment. Then he approached the lad, saying abruptly, " I'm going to horse-whip you, young McRoss."

Hiram's face flushed crimson with shame, but Mr. Grant's keen eyes saw not a trace of anger.

" Have you anything to urge why I shouldn't flog you ? "

" No, sir, nothing," replied Hiram, humbly ; and he stretched out his hands to receive the punishment. The surprise and relief of the Principal were great. He had fully intended to make Hiram take off his coat, but concluded at once to inflict the stripes in the way the lad evidently expected them.

" Young McRoss," said the master, sadly, " I am *very* sorry to have to punish you so severely. If you think I am giving you too much will you tell me ? "

" I can *trust* you, Mr. Grant."

The Principal's voice trembled as he said " My boy, I would not intentionally be over-severe; but never having flogged anyone before, it is possible to make a mistake. If I whip you too hard, young McRoss, tell me and I will stop at once."

" Just as you wish, sir. But, Mr. Grant—my hands are soft—they will be easily cut—and you must not mind *that*."

The Principal immediately commenced to inflict the

punishment. He knew that, to do good, it must be no child's play—and *it was not*. The whip cut up Hiram's hands more and more deeply at every stroke; the lash was stained red, and the blood trickled from his fingers on to the floor. Still the master did not stop, and Hiram's rosy face grew white with pain, but he uttered no cry, made no complaint. At last, Mr. Grant put down the whip, saying, tenderly, " That will do, young McRoss." The wounded hands dropped, and Hiram came closer to the Principal, who sorrowfully said, " So this is your *first* flogging, my boy ! "

" Yes, sir ; and I *thank* you for it ! " The lad's eyes, as he looked up, were bright and tearless.

"My brave boy," said the Principal, and he put his arm around young McRoss and kissed him. Hiram could not stand *that*, but burst out crying. His hands were bleeding. so he did not cover his face but laid it against Mr. Grant's breast.

" Young McRoss, indeed I did not mean to hurt your feelings."

" You have not, sir. It was worth being flogged to get that kiss."

" You foolish child," said the Principal, smiling, as he clasped his arms closer around Hiram. " I kiss you every night, but you are asleep and don't know it."

" Oh, Mr. Grant! I'll keep awake after this ! " Hiram's voice was choked with sobs.

" No—no—that will never do ! You are nearly always asleep by eleven o'clock ; otherwise, I do not disturb you." And the Principal stroked Hiram's curly hair and gently dried his tears.

"Dear Mr. Grant, you are very good to forgive me and care for me still," sobbed Hiram. "Indeed, I *do* love you, though I acted so badly."

"Not more than I love *you*, my precious young McRoss, you are dearer to me than ever." And the Principal kissed Hiram again, which was followed by another burst of crying.

As soon as he was quieted the master released him, and Hiram immediately went out to his comrades and showed them his bleeding hands. He forgot that his face was swollen with crying. On similar occasions he had taken good care to keep out of the way until all traces of emotion were past. But now, in his eagerness to vindicate the honour of the Principal he lost all thought of himself.

"You said that Mr. Grant would be unjust, Thorne. Take back your words, please," said Hiram.

"I take them back. He is *not* unjust, but *very cruel*. I would rather be expelled a dozen times over than suffer like that." And George turned away, feeling sick and faint at the sight.

The lads were bitterly indignant. Mr. Slow, who happened to be among them, said that his superior had acted barbarously. Hiram defended the Principal with even more than his customary warmth. As soon as the lad's back was turned, his comrades roundly denounced Mr. Grant as a brute. Their fun was spoiled, and Giovanni remarked, "the boys are not going to play any more. Thorne, would you like a story book to read?"

"Yes, if there is nothing better to do."

"Then, come to my room and choose one."

The two lads went upstairs into Giovanni's apartment. "Oh! that horrible picture," exclaimed Thorne, hastily passing it. "Why, you have got quite a nice library here. Let me see 'Ten Nights in a Bar-room,' is that interesting?"

"Yes," responded Giovanni, coolly; "but, *you* would not like it, it is about dreadful things, and your nerves don't seem very strong."

"You disagreeable little fright."

Giovanni coloured, but made no reply.

"I take that back," said Thorne. "Your features are not girlish, like Shuter's, but, *I* prefer them to *his*. When quite a child I was frightened almost to death by an odious nurse-girl, and my nerves are scarcely over it yet. Don't play tricks on me!"

"I have something else to do."

"What?"

"*Fight rum*," said Giovanni Somerville.

George smiled. "I don't know which book to choose. Pick one out yourself."

His companion did so.

"Thank you. Are all those forty, or so, odd volumes, Temperance books?"

"Every single one."

"What good are they?"

"Good! Why they help forward *the Cause*. All the boys have read some of them, mostly the stories. Your friend Tom won't read anything else, but they have done him good, for, he is strong in the glorious Cause of Temperance."

"I'll follow Tom's example and read the stories. I suppose that you prefer the 'Text Book of Temperance,' and kindred works?"

"Yes."

"What are you going to make of yourself?"

"I hope to be a Temperance Lecturer."

"I might have guessed as much," laughed Thorne. "How can you sleep with those horrid creatures glaring at you?" he asked more gravely.

"Why, there are lots of demons in our poor, lost world. We can't see them, that is all. There are, no doubt, some *here*, at this moment, and far more terrible looking than those in the picture."

Thorne turned pale. "So, *you* are not afraid?"

"No, George, of course not. I'm in Christ's arms, and all the demons in hell can never get me out."

There was silence. Soon Thorne caught sight of a handsome Bible, bound in scarlet morocco. "*That's* not a Temperance book!" he observed, with a smile.

Giovanni's large brown eyes opened wide as he exclaimed, "Not a Temperance Book! Why, Thorne, you know better than that. The blessed Bible is the strongest Temperance book in the world."

George laughed. He feared defeat, should he try an

argument with his total abstinence companion. What, if all the important facts in that formidable array of literature before his eyes were safely stowed away in his young friend's brain! It was not at all unlikely. "I'll not risk it, any way;" thought Thorne to himself, as he went down stairs.

After expressing his utter disapproval of Mr. Grant's "barbarity" to that gentleman himself, the assistant continued, "If you flog any of the other lads so shamefully the parents will bring a law-suit against you—ay, and gain it, too."

Mr. Grant drew himself up proudly, "Do you suppose I would *trouble* myself to flog one of the others? No indeed; I would expel the whole of them first. Not young McRoss, though, I cannot spare *him.*"

At the tea-table Mr. Slow inquired "Why did you not flog Hiram over his shoulders? He will not be able to touch a snowball for a week to come."

"I intended to have made him take off his coat," said the Principal.

Hiram's cheeks flushed. "Oh, Mr. Grant, indeed I never thought of that! Why didn't you tell me?"

"You held out your hands before I was ready, young McRoss," said the Principal, with a smile.

The assistant gravely inquired, "Did the master soon make you cry, Hiram?"

The head teacher replied, "Young McRoss was a brave boy. After receiving the last stroke he was no more crying, Mr. Slow, than you are now."

The assistant and scholars looked surprised. "He cried about something," said Shuter. "What was it, Hiram?"

"Mr. Grant's kindness made a baby of me, Aleck." Hiram's face crimsoned as he made the confession, and the assistant and lads laughed.

"None of the other scholars could have borne such a flogging so bravely," said Mr. Slow.

"Nor the assistant either," added Shuter.

"I don't know about *that*," growled Mr. Slow.

When the lads returned to the school-room, George managed to get McRoss to himself, and enquired, "How can you care for Mr. Grant now?"

"*I love him more dearly than ever!*"

"I don't understand at all. Is there anyone that you love *better* than the Principal?"

"Yes—*One*," replied Hiram McRoss.

"And who is that?" asked George.

"The Lord Jesus," answered his companion, reverently.

George was taken by surprise. He said, at length, "I don't wonder at *that*. But *why* do you like the head teacher?"

"*He* taught me to love Jesus," said Hiram, in a low, deep voice, as though his very soul were stirred. "Yes, George, next to my Saviour, I have *good* reason to love Mr. Grant."

"McRoss!" called the assistant. "my superior wants to see you."

Hiram went off at once to the library-parlour, and was

locked in alone with the Principal. That gentleman took the wounded hands in his own, and was shocked to see that nothing had been applied to heal the cuts.

"I did not think that you would like it, sir."

"Poor child! I wish I had known; you must have suffered acutely all the afternoon. I will dress them myself now." And so he did, most tenderly. Hiram looked towards the books which were laid beside the Principal and sorrowfully said, as the dressing was finished, "I have kept you from those favourite studies so long, sir. My hands feel much better now."

"It is well they do; but don't trouble yourself about the books, young McRoss, I am going to keep you all the evening. Take the corner of the lounge or that low rocking-chair—or sit anywhere you please."

Hiram, colouring deeply, seated himself on Mr. Grant's knee. That gentleman laughed, and put his strong arms around his favourite.

"You think I'm a big baby, sir, and no wonder; but if you're going to scold me I want to come close."

"I'm not going to scold you, child, but you may come as close as you choose."

Hiram immediately took him at his word, and Mr. Grant caressingly stroked the curly head that lay on his breast.

"Young McRoss, will you tell me about your early life?" asked the Principal.

"I'm afraid it will weary you, sir."

"Go ahead, my boy, there is no danger."

"I must tell you the first part, then, as I have heard it from Aunt Ellen. Father was a sailor from boyhood, but he gave up the sea for the sake of my mother, who, Aunt says, was a very pretty girl, with bright curly hair and blue eyes. They married and settled down on a farm, which belonged to her. A year afterwards I was born, and, as a baby, father almost hated me, because I cost the life of his idolized Lily. He went off to the sea again, and left me to the care of Aunt Ellen, who thought it sinful to punish a motherless child, and allowed me to do as I chose. I used to tease and slap the servants, but they did not dare to touch me in return. Father came home about every two years, but *he* never punished me either. If I had taken after mother he would have had me with him at sea long ago; but he could not help seeing that I was the picture of himself, and, moreover, inherited his hot temper as well. So he said I might please myself, which I did, and went to school instead of becoming a sailor. The master at Oakville is a great friend of aunt's, and that is why I escaped punishment until coming here. Father wished me to go to sea with him the last time he was home. He has been a captain for eight years now, and promised me good times; but I did not like the thought, so he would not urge me. Of course, I should always make him think of his dead wife; but, for that matter, he has her life-size picture hanging up in his cabin. Aunt Nelly dares not mention her sister's name, for, even yet, Captain McRoss will cry like a child over his 'lost Lily.' He often said what a pity it was that *I* did not die instead of mother, and lately I have sometime thought so myself."

" Why, young McRoss!"

" It is so discouraging, sir. It seems as if it is no good to fight against my bad temper any longer. Father says, I got it from him; but, instead of breaking me of it, they give it full swing. I never tried to control it until I came here; and it seems almost useless to struggle against it now. I *do* love Christ, though I am nothing but a shame to Him!" and Hiram burst into tears.

· Mr. Grant answered, in a low, soothing tone, "*He* knows all, my child. You must ask your Saviour's forgiveness, young McRoss, and He will enable you to do better. Never fear! You shall come off '*more* than conqueror through Him who loved you.'"

"He *has* forgiven me, sir;" said Hiram, in a broken voice, "and I'm so glad that you have too. Dear Mr. Grant, *you* taught me to love Jesus. Under God, I owe everything to you, both in this world and the world to come!"

There was no answer; and, when Hiram looked up, he saw tears rolling down the face of the Principal. The lad laid his head on the master's breast, as before, while Mr. Grant, hugging him close, said huskily, " I did not think you could have made *me* cry, young McRoss!"

" I am very sorry, sir, to have given you pain."

" You have given me the purest pleasure. You are *my own child* now; mine for ever and ever! Look upon

C

me as your father after this; for, by your own confession, I *am* your father, young McRoss."

Then, the Principal arose; and, making Hiram kneel down beside him, commended himself and his spiritual son, the child that God had given him, into the hands of their dear Lord and Saviour. When they arose from their knees, Hiram was crying more than ever. He thought he had very good reason. Mr. Grant, however, was quite calm, and took Hiram in his arms again, petting him like a child, until he was more composed. He then inquired, " Young McRoss, are you really fond of intoxicating liquors ?"

" Yes, sir; but, God helping me, I will keep my pledge. I got the taste for rum from my father—it is hereditary in *him*, much more so in *me*, for father is a hard drinker. He taught me to sip grog from his tumbler when I was a little child."

"I am thankful indeed that you have signed the pledge!"

"And, so am I, sir. It did not strike me as of much importance until last night, when Giovanni was so distressed on my account, that, for the first time, I gave the matter serious thought. It is not likely, though, that I would have signed the pledge, unless you had made me. I had not the slightest intention of doing it, though I had made up my mind to be more careful in future."

The lads saw nothing of Hiram, until it was time for prayers, when he came in with Mr. Grant. They noticed that he had been crying again. The temporary emotion of the Principal had left no trace. Hiram went up stairs to the little room, which he occupied alone; but, no sooner was his head laid on the pillow, than the Principal came in, stroked back his favourite's curly hair and "young McRoss" was delighted by receiving the usual goodnight kiss on his forehead, when he was *awake*, instead of *asleep*.

CHAPTER IV.

" SUNDAY AT THE SEMINARY."

"O, this is my first Sunday at Roseville Seminary;" thought George Thorne, as he looked listlessly around the school-room. He saw that Giovanni was at his desk,· perusing a large volume, very intently. The new scholar approached and inquired, "What are you reading?"

"A commentary."

"I thought that you read precious little of anything, except Teetotal Literature;" said George.

Giovanni smiled so strangely, that Thorne was impelled by curiosity to examine the volume for himself. Then, he burst out laughing and exclaimed " *Temperance Bible*

Commentary: I might have guessed as much. Well, enjoy it in peace:" and George marched off.

"What are *you* about, Ivon?"

"I'm learning the Articles;" said the ten-year old.

"You are beginning in good time;" remarked Thorne merrily. "There's Giovanni over yonder, studying Teetotalism; and, here are you, commencing your ministerial duties."

"Of course;" replied Ivon, "Giovanni's work is different from either Archie's or mine; not, but that *we* would inculcate Temperance, whenever we get a chance; only, we don't expect to be professional lecturers on the subject, as *he* does. We are all employed by the same Master What is *your* work, Thorne; and *how* are you doing it?"

George looked very uncomfortable, and Tom seeing it, came up and drew his friend away. They stood at a window, talking in the most idle manner, for half an hour, when George remarked, "I believe that Hiram McRoss finds more pleasure in reading the Bible than we do in talking nonsense. Just see him now; where could you find a more happy-looking face?"

"Wasn't he happy-looking yesterday," sneered Tom, "when his face was swollen with crying?"

"Now, that's too bad;" answered George, hotly. He stopped short; for Hiram came up and said gently, "Mr. Grant does not wish us to waste the Sabbath, Thorne; and, *you* know it is not right."

"Walk off, Mr. Hiram;" said Tom, "*you* have no business to interfere. Just remember what a sweet example you set us yesterday."

"It *was*, Tom," replied George, angrily. "I know I couldn't follow it. If Mr. Grant flogged *me* so cruelly, I would curse him to his face."

"You had better not, Thorne;" returned Hiram, excitedly. " Your curses would return upon your own head; Not one jot of the evil, you wished on him, could ever come to pass. Mr. Grant is one of those, of whom the Bible says, ' Blessed is he that blesseth thee ; and *cursed is he that curseth thee.'* "

George shuddered, but made no reply.

Hiram went on, in a different tone, " I should be sorry for you to copy *me*, Tom. The example I set, yesterday, was a very bad one."

The words of McRoss had sufficient influence with Thorne, to cause him to take a Sunday book and read it until church-time. Then the lads assembled in the hall, and the two teachers soon made their appearance.

"There's to be a sermon preached in the Temperance Hall, at Roseville, uncle. Oh, do go, so as to give me a chance of hearing it. Mr. Grant will not trust any of us alone."

" How tiresome you are, nephew."

" *I* would like to go ; " remarked George.

"Very well. Then, I'll go, *this* time;" said Mr. Slow.

" You *may*, and welcome ; " replied his superior, gravely, " and take your nephew, as well ; but, Thorne and the other lads will have to go with me. I cannot trust them out of my sight."

" *I* can take care of them," snarled the assistant.

"Possibly you might, sir; if you could only keep awake; but, that seems a difficult matter," said Mr. Grant, drily.

Mr. Slow frowned as he remarked; "I wonder that you will consent to let my nephew go."

"Oh," said the Principal, "Temperance is Giovanni's study and delight! There is no doubt that *he* will behave himself, even though you sleep through the entire sermon."

"I fully intend to, if it is at all *dry*"; replied Mr. Slow, angrily.

"If you wish, I'll keep nudging you, uncle."

"I'll box your ears, if you do."

At the dinner table, Thorne inquired of the assistant "if the Teetotal sermon was interesting.'

"No—(now, you needn't stare, Giovanni!) at least, the first part was dry, and I did not hear the rest of it!"

"Where was the good of your going at all?"

"I went on my nephew's account, Mr. Grant. Besides, I *did* listen, at first; but, the man began to speak about ghosts; and then, truly, I thought it was high time to get to sleep; for, I firmly believe in them already; though, much to my own discomfort."

"Did the preacher believe in them?" asked Thorne, with wide-open eyes.

"No, no;" replied Giovanni. "He says that if any people on earth are haunted by ghosts, it is the rumsellers. He also assured us that if it is not so in this life, it will in the life to come!"

"Certainly," replied Archie; "unless they repent."

"Then I'll *never* be a rumseller!" exclaimed George Thorne.

"And so *you* liked it, Giovanni?"

"Yes, Horace. It was interesting—*painfully* interesting. Mr. Grant, (addressing that gentleman), "there was something in it so shocking to me, so strange as well; would you mind saying if·it is true or not?"

"I am no judge, Giovanni, of anything pertaining to the subject—not being at all posted in temperance matters."

"It's high time you were, sir."

"My nephew, be careful what you say."

"Well!" exclaimed Giovanni, rising up, excitedly, "it *is* high time he was. Now, on one side, there are the total-abstinence bands—on the other, the forces of liquordom. There is no neutrality. You must be on one side or the other. *God* is the leader of the temperance army; while Satan is the friend and ally of the rumsellers. And does any man in his senses dare to tell me that it is of trifling importance whether he is 'posted' in these matters or not? What! Not posted concerning the progress of the war now raging between the hosts of light and the powers of darkness? Oh, Mr. Grant—Mr. Grant! You are doing good in other ways; good with your time —good with your money; but why look so coldly upon the Total Abstinence movement? *Why* just save yourself and calmly allow others to perish? Uncle says he has often seen you give so willingly and largely to missionary and bible societies; but, did you ever give a dollar to the temperance cause ? And yet drunkenness is ruining more souls than all other crimes put together. Where is the good of sending out missionaries with Bibles and tracts when the very same vessel carries in her hold hogsheads of rum to the hapless heathen? *You* have influence, learning, position, wealth—and for all these talents you are accountable. Oh, why won't you 'come up to the help of the Lord; to the help of the Lord, against the mighty?' "

The teachers and scholars were too much surprised to make any immediate reply. At length the assistant said earnestly, " Giovanni, Giovanni, *do* sit down and get your dinner."

"Excuse me, uncle, if you please," replied the boy, as he went off to his own room. Pacing the floor, in his excitement, he said aloud, "May God forgive me if I spoke disrespectfully to Mr. Grant. I didn't mean to; but, oh, he has been asleep all these years; *wilfully* asleep in regard to temperance. The Principal took good care to save *himself* from a drunkard's grave; he mounted the rock of total abstinence; but what unfortunate creatures has he pulled up beside him, during all these twenty years? From his own confession, *not one*, until yesterday, when I am sure that *God* must have touched his cold heart, or he would never have pledged himself—no, not even to save Hiram McRoss."

When the meal was over, and the lads were alone again, Thorne remarked, "What a strange thing! I thought Giovanni was so quiet."

"He is, *generally,*" said Archie. "If he did wrong, it was an error of judgment, and nothing more——"

"Giovanni took a different pledge from ours," said Aieck. "You will never hear of it from himself, Thorne; but when you get a chance of looking in his Bible, you will find it *there,* as *I* did, when meddling with what did not belong to me."

George laughed, and inwardly hoped that Shuter would keep out of *his* room.

"There is no doubt, on my mind, that Giovanni acted quite right," said Horace Raymond. "If the proud, reserved head-teacher does not take care, he will remember that passionate appeal, with sorrow, in the judgment day."

"*Never!*" hotly returned Hiram McRoss. "To *know* duty is to *do* it, with Mr. Grant! Is it so with *you,* Horace?"

Raymond coloured as he replied, "not always."

"Neither is it with *me,*" said Hiram, sorrowfully. "Oh, Horace, I wish that we were as sure of our crowns as Mr. Grant is."

In the meantime, conscience was whispering to the head-teacher that he had not done his duty in regard to the temperance cause; but, for a great wonder, he proudly refused to listen to it. Therefore he was not in a very happy frame of mind when he appeared before his scholars to conduct the Bible class. The intended lesson seemed to have slipped from his memory; but just at that moment he caught sight of the hands of Hiram McRoss, who always sat close beside him. The thought of his favourite fighting—fighting all the way through from earth to heaven, flashed across his mind, and his pride gave way. Bowing his head on his hands he prayed in his heart, "Lord Jesus, forgive me. Shew me what *Thou* would'st have me to do, and, by Thy grace, I will do it." When he raised his head, Hiram laid his hand gently on the master's arm, saying sorrowfully, "Oh, Mr. Grant, don't teach us if you have one of those dreadful headaches."

"I am very well, child," said the Principal, gravely. He then opened the Bible Class with prayer, as usual, and, afterwards, said to the lads, "You may each repeat a hymn all around. I'll begin with *you*, young McRoss.

Hiram's choice was, "Am I a soldier of the Cross," etc. Then the lads took it in turn, until it came to Giovanni, who respectfully inquired, "You won't object to a Temperance hymn, sir?"

"No; do you know any others?" asked Mr. Grant, coolly; which question set several of the boys grinning.

"Yes, sir, perhaps you would prefer *this*:

" Dare to be right ! Dare to be true !
You have a work that no other can do ;
Do it so bravely, so kindly, so well,
As to gladden all Heaven, and silence all Hell.

" Dare to be right ! Dare to be true !
Other men's failures can never save you ;
Stand by your conscience, your honour, your faith ;
Stand like a hero, and battle till death.

"SUNDAY AT THE SEMINARY." 51

" Dare to be right ! Dare to be true !
God, who created you, cares for you, too ;
Treasures the tears that His striving ones shed,
Counts and protects every hair of your head.

" Dare to be right ! Dare to be true !
Cannot Omnipotence carry you through ?
City and mansion and throne all in sight,
Can you not dare to be true and be right ?

" Dare to be right ! Dare to be true !
Keep the great Judgment Seat always in view ;
Look at your work as you'll look at it then,
Scanned by Jehovah and angels and men.

" Dare to be right ! Dare to be true !
Prayerfully, lovingly, firmly pursue
The pathway by saints and by seraphim trod,
The pathway that climbs to the City of God."

The hymn went home to the hearts of Iyon, Archie and several others, it soothed the excited feelings of the Principal ; it cheered Hiram McRoss ; it aroused anew the conscience of George Thorne ; and it thrilled through and through the soul of the young Temperance advocate, as he repeated the brave inspiriting words. The lads looked at Giovanni's lighted-up countenance, and regarded him as a hero ; but, the boy was in blissful ignorance of it ; *he* was hoping that Mr. Grant would take the hymn to himself, and become an earnest worker in the ranks of the Teetotallers. It took some time for the scholars to finish their pieces ; and then, the Principal, beginning *not* with Hiram, but at the other end of the class, ordered each of them to repeat a verse from Scripture. At length it came to Giovanni.

"*He* will give us a Temperance text," thought Mr. Grant, but that worthy gentleman was mistaken. Not even glancing at the master, so as to insinuate any allusion to him, but looking calmly into the blue eyes of Archie Campbell, Giovanni repeated in a clear voice that rang through the room, " Curse ye Meroz, said the angel of the Lord, curse ye bitterly the inhabitants thereof; because they came not to the help of the Lord, to the help of the Lord against the mighty."

The head teacher winced at the home-thrust; poor Mr. Slow hurried out of the room, sure that his situation was gone for good; the lads were astonished at the boldness of their comrade; but when Hiram saw the flushed face of the Principal, he hotly exclaimed, " Won't you turn Giovanni out of the room, sir? "

" Oh, no, young McRoss," said Mr. Grant, with a smile.

The recitation went on, until it came to Hiram who repeated earnestly, " They that be wise shall shine as the brightness of the firmament; and they that turn many to righteousness as the stars for ever and ever.—Behold I and the children which God hath given me."

The scholars smiled; they knew well that Hiram intended the verses for the head teacher. That gentleman arose, and saying gravely, "Thank you, young McRoss," leaned down and pressed his lips to the boy's forehead, in a warm fatherly kiss. Then, abruptly saying to the class, "You are dismissed," he left the room.

"You are a real hero, Giovanni," said Tom.

His comrade's pale cheeks reddened as he replied impatiently, "I'm nothing of the kind, nor ever will be. Keep your nonsense to yourself, Tom."

"What a queer Bible-class," said Thorne.

"Oh, George," remarked Ivon, "it is not often as we had it to-day. *We* never know where the lesson is— sometimes it's a Psalm, sometimes a doctrine, parable or miracle, sometimes hymns and verses. He is an eccentric teacher, certainly; I don't think he knows what is to be the next lesson, himself."

"What was the question with which you entrapped the Principal, so finely?" asked Thorne of his Temperance comrade.

"I did not *mean* to entrap him," replied Giovanni earnestly, "and if he would have listened to me, I have no doubt that he could have answered it all right, for it requires Christian knowledge and common sense, and he has any amount of both."

"Perhaps Archie can help you," said Ivon.

"I'll try him," returned Giovanni. "You see the lecturer read various extracts from different sources, in the course of his remarks; and, I took one or two of them down. *This* is what I wished to ask Mr. Grant—now Archie, is it true?" And Giovanni read as follows:

"I might dwell upon this subject. I might shew you that everything in grace is founded in nature, so there is no evil so great as that which destroys, even for a time, the integrity of our nature ; because it destroys the possibility of grace. Every other sinner might cry out to God and get grace, get forgiveness, get redemption. The drunkard alone, is incapable of sending forth that cry. We have the dreadful truth before us—that if the Son of God came down from Heaven and stood over the drunkard, Omnipotent as He is, He could do nothing for him."

"Now," said Giovanni, "did you ever hear anything so shocking ? The blessed Lord Jesus Himself powerless to save the drunkard, so long as that drunkard continues in his insensible state."

"It is indeed a fearful thought;" replied Archie Campbell, " I wish you had asked Mr. Grant."

Soon, Mr. Slow entered, and remarked, " My nephew, I greatly feared you had lost my situation for me; but, happily, it is not so. *Do* be careful!"

"Indeed, uncle, I meant to act right. You know that, for three years, I have tried hard to *persuade* Mr. Grant to become a Temperance worker."

"I think you have managed it at last, Giovanni!" and Mr. Slow laughed.

"I would like to box your nephew's ears, sir ;" said Hiram, warmly. "If he ever gets to be the one-thousandth part as good as Mr. Grant is, you will have great reason to be thankful!"

"There is some sense in what you say, *Mr.* Hiram;" snarled the assistant, whose conscience compelled him to speak up for the head-master. "My superior does much good with his wealth—and, as secretly as possible. At the Great Day, there will, doubtless, be hundreds at Christ's right hand, who would not have been there, but for the instrumentality of Mr. Grant. He *is* cold and reserved; but, he took after his stern, Puritan father, and *not* after his butterfly mother—any *blind* body could see that! He does not choose to make you apologize, Giovanni; but, freely acknowledges it would have been better if he *had* read some standard Temperance books and done something for the cause you have so much at heart. I am sure that if anyone is actuated, in his daily life, by the love of Christ, it is the head-teacher!"

Then, Mr. Slow departed, and Tom mockingly inquired, " Did Mr. Grant ever kiss you before, Hiram ?"

" Yes ;" answered the lad, calmly.

" Aren't you ashamed ?" asked Reynolds.

" Ashamed!" repeated Hiram, in surprise : "I was never so proud of anything in my life!"

After some further bantering remarks, Tom impatiently inquired, " Is it impossible to put you out of temper?"

" I trust so," replied McRoss, gravely ; " at least, about such a subject as Mr. Grant's kisses!"

CHAPTER V.

"TEMPERANCE ON THE BRAIN."

THE next morning, at breakfast, Mr. Slow snappishly inquired, " Was not the Principal vexed with you for crying, Hiram; as it's a thing he is never guilty of himself? Now, you needn't stare at me, with those black eyes, which are just the counterparts of Mr. Grant's! Perhaps you don't believe what I say!"

Hiram's face crimsoned; but he did not reply.

" Do you suppose the master is ever guilty of crying?" persisted Mr. Slow.

No answer.

" You obstinate fellow! Just confess I am right. A stone would shed tears before Mr. Grant would!"

Then, McRoss thought fit to speak. " That is not true, sir; and you know it."

" Answer my question directly, you bad boy!"

" I don't intend to do anything of the kind."

" You're a stubborn, good-for-nothing lad," commenced the assistant, but he was stopped by Mr. Grant, who said, gravely, " That will do, Mr. Slow. Young McRoss succeeded in making me cry last Saturday night; therefore, he cannot agree with you."

The lads looked as much astonished as the assistant, who snarled out, "What do you suppose your scholars will think of you now, sir? It is very disgraceful and unmanly to cry!"

The boys laughed; they were highly pleased; but the face of the Principal was painfully flushed.

"It is *not* unmanly to cry!" exclaimed Hiram hotly, "and it's *not* disgraceful! How dare you say so, Mr. Slow?"

"Young McRoss!" said the Principal, gravely.

"Yes, sir;" said Hiram, in as different a tone as possible, so gentle and respectful, that Thorne was amazed at the sudden change.

"You may take my part, if you wish; but, keep your temper, my boy."

"I'll *try*, sir:" replied Hiram. Then, turning to the assistant, he went on, "Of course, in many cases it is childish to cry—I am not defending myself—but, the tears that Mr. Grant spoke of, were such as an angel might have shed; and, for you to condemn *all* crying, as unmanly and disgraceful, is downright wicked. How dare you say so, when the only perfect man that ever lived even our Lord Jesus Christ—*cried*!"

Hiram's words brought a sudden gravity and silence at the table. The assistant and all the scholars felt that McRoss had taken the Principal's part with a vengeance; and, in a way, that it was impossible to answer. The master felt it, too, and the look of loving approval, which he bestowed, went to the heart of "young McRoss."

When Mr. Grant walked to Roseville, that afternoon, as usual he ordered a number of solid temperance books;

D

being determined to "post" himself on the subject without further delay. George Thorne, meanwhile, stole softly into Giovanni's room, hastily took up his Bible and found the Pledge, which was pasted on the cover inside. It was written neatly, in Giovanni's unmistakable school boy hand. George read.

"TEMPERANCE PLEDGE.

"Through Christ, who strengtheneth me, I promise to abstain for ever, from all intoxicating liquor. And I hereby devote myself, body and soul, to the good of the Temperance Cause. So help me, God!

"GIOVANNI SOMERVILLE."

With a very grave face, Thorne closed the book and went down stairs. From Shuter he learned that the first part of *that* Pledge was copied from a story, which was published in the *Montreal Witness;* but that the latter part was probably a thought of Giovanni's own.

"What are you reading, my assistant?" asked Mr. Grant, on his return from Roseville.

"You may well inquire, sir. It's a nasty, dry book, which my nephew made me promise to read; but, I *hate* it —— so I do."

The Principal laughed and examined the volume. "It's on Temperance, of course;" he said.

"Yes, Temperance and religion, together; Giovanni has read it through three times," and Mr. Slow stalked out of the room.

"Thorne, my old friend, what is the matter with you, to-night?" asked Tom.

"*That Pledge*," replied George. "What a solemn thing —it has rung in my ears ever since. 'I hereby devote myself, body and soul, to the good of the Temperance Cause.' Right nobly is Giovanni fulfilling his vow! And, what am I doing? Nothing. Ivon asked me, on Sunday, 'What is *your* work, Thorne; and how are you doing it?' Why, I am not even a Christian; and, if I die to-night, I am lost."

"My dear fellow, you are nervous. Has that Archie been talking to you?" he added, angrily.

"Yes, as lovingly as my mother ever did. He is very anxious to be a missionary."

"I heartily wish he was one, now; and far away from Roseville Seminary!"

"*I* don't. Oh, dear—oh, dear!"

"Come, old fellow, you'll sleep this off," said Tom.

The next morning, Mr. Slow inquired, "What made you come here just before vacation, George?"

Thorne coloured. "I—I—" he began, and suddenly stopped. "I was very sick at home, for some months, and just came to see how I should like it."

"Do you intend to come back?"

"Of course, he does," answered Tom. But when they were alone, he said, "I wonder you durst say that, George. It is well the Principal does not know that you were turned out of the other Institution. Aren't you afraid of a flogging?"

" *Yes*, that's why I said it. Oh, I wish I was as brave as Hiram McRoss!"

All that day, the words of Archie and Ivon troubled the new-comer; and Giovanni's Pledge still rang in his ears; but it seemed no use wishing to be a Christian; for, after that lie, Heaven was farther off than ever to poor George Thorne.

And now, the day for breaking up arrived. The lads were talking in the school-room, early, when Tom and others expressed their regret that Giovanni was not going away to —— " to have a good time."

The lad's eyes brightened with sudden fire; and he exclaimed in the greatest excitement, " There's a good time coming, boys : *yes, a good time coming*, when there won't be a grog-shop or a rumseller in the land!"

The scholars looked amused. Giovanni spoke again, but, in his usual calm tone. "How many of you will do me a favour?"

" All of us," replied Tom.

" Well," said their comrade, eagerly, " I want you all to promise to do what you can to advance the cause of Temperance, during vacation."

There was a general smile. " *I'll* not promise," returned George ; " we haven't all got ' Temperance on the brain,' as *you* have!"

" Temperance on the brain," repeated Giovanni, bitterly. " No, *Temperance on the heart.*" He then added in the same tone, but in a broken voice, " had you seen *your* father die, Thorne—die in terrible agony of delirium tremens, as *mine* did, you would not have said that." Giovanni turned away. He was a brave little fellow; but, it was hard to control his emotion, when the memories of events, that had saddened his young life, came over him. Thorne's conscience bitterly reproached him; he felt that it was useless to offer any excuse. Giovanni soon recovered his composure and asked, " Won't any of you promise ?"

Nearly all agreed to *try*, at least.

At breakfast, Ivon remarked, " We are all glad of the holidays, except Hiram McRoss."

" He is sorry to leave Mr. Grant, I suppose," sneered the assistant. " My superior is away a great deal in vacation-times. So many possessions need considerable looking after. Now, Hiram, don't you wish you had one of Mr. Grant's farms ?"

" No, sir; I shall have a farm of my own, on coming of age," calmly replied the lad.

" Is there a house on it ?" inquired the assistant, in a tone of surprise.

" Oh, yes, sir," laughed Hiram. " Do you suppose we live in a barn ? There is a brick house on it; one of the large, old-fashioned kind."

" Of course, your relatives expect you to work the place as soon as you are twenty-one ?"

" Yes, sir."

" Oh, young McRoss," said Mr. Grant, sorrowfully, " it is hard to lose you so soon."

" I don't intend to be a farmer, sir."

"What, then?" growled Mr. Slow.

"I don't know," replied Hiram, gloomily.

"You're a lucky fellow," said Tom, "and now, you need not be troubled; for, as you have property of your own, on coming of age, you can stay with Mr. Grant until you are thirty years old, or longer, if you choose. But, the Principal will very likely die before that!"

"I hope that *I* shall die too, then!" replied Hiram.

Mr. Slow looked dreadfully shocked.

"Is that a right wish, young McRoss?"

There was a tremor in the Principal's usually calm voice.

"Yes, sir; I think so. I pray for it every day. It cannot be wrong to hope that my prayer will be answered."

"How fearfully dangerous to say such prayers!" exclaimed the assistant.

"Not at all, sir. I always ask 'if it be God's will.' Innocent wishes, like that, have been so often granted by our loving Saviour, that I think He will grant *mine!*" and Hiram smiled.

The Principal arose hastily and left the room. McRoss quickly followed him into the parlour and locked the door, for, he saw that Mr. Grant was crying like a child. Hiram clasped his arms around the master, saying sorrowfully, "Dear Mr. Grant, I did not mean to hurt you!" The Principal raised his head and took Hiram in his arms, hugging him closely to his breast. The lad was shocked to find that the master had lost all control of his feelings, and was sobbing and crying in a manner that would have alarmed Mr. Slow, had he witnessed it. Hiram lay still, with his curly head on Mr. Grant's bosom. He felt the hot tears fall upon his face; and longed—oh, how he longed to comfort the Principal. It was useless to speak until the storm was over. At last the master became more calm, and kissed Hiram again and again. "My dear young McRoss," he said in a faltering tone, " you had better not say that prayer any more!"

"Why not, sir?" asked Hiram, in surprise.

"My child, I am just forty years old, while you are not quite twenty, and, I trust, have a long, happy life before you. From the nature of things, I cannot expect to live as long as yourself—do you really wish to shorten your days?"

"I would like to die with you, sir, if God be willing, even though death came to-day or to-morrow; and, I shall pray for it now, more than ever!" replied Hiram earnestly.

Before the lad left Mr. Grant, he asked pardon for coming in so unceremoniously.

"You are welcome to go all over the house, whenever you please, young McRoss."

"Thank you, sir," replied Hiram gratefully, "I often wished to come in here, when you had those fearful headaches."

Mr. Grant smiled. "I am sorry that I did not know it before," he said.

When Hiram got back to his companions, Mr. Slow was saying, "Yes, lads—the Principal's boyhood was a cold, cheerless one. His gay, fashionable mother cared not for either husband or child; and, finally left both, simply because she could not attend balls, theatres, etc., every night in the week! Her parents upheld her in such folly—much to their regret afterwards, for she died soon after she went home to them; died of pneumonia—contracted one bitterly cold night, when she attended the theatre in laces and frippery. I don't wonder that my superior has a feeling akin to dislike towards all woman-folks, when his father's marriage was such an unhappy one. The said father was a reserved, stern man, who gave his son plenty of the rod, but very little love with it. So the boy grew up without that affection for his parents which nearly all children have. He was the only child, and his father died when he was twelve years old—his mother, long before that. The Principal inherited his father's peculiar temperament; *that* kept him from forming friendships either at school or college; however, he has no reason to complain, for, from his boyhood, he has had a Friend in Heaven—which is more than I have—"

" O, Mr. Slow, Jesus would—"

" Just stop, Archie," growled the assistant, "I know what you would say. Well, Mr. Grant has had a lonely life! He has superintended this Seminary for eighteen years, and never even cared to make a favourite, until Hiram came and took his cold heart by storm! I learned those facts about my superior's early life from an old lawyer (an American) who was here some time ago. I guess," concluded Mr. Slow with a laugh, " that Mr

Grant won't be lonely any longer, for, he is evidently going to make a pet and plaything of that big Hiram McRoss."

Archie smiled. "Hiram isn't big, sir, and never will be—but, he is one of the eldest of us."

"Do you call him little?"

"Oh, no, Mr. Slow. He is as tall as yourself; but in, comparison of Mr. Grant—"

"Hurrah!" exclaimed Shuter, "there's the omnibus!"

CHAPTER VI.

THE HOLIDAYS.

"DON'T you think that Hiram has changed very much, Sam, during the past year?"

"Yes, indeed, Miss Morris."

"The idea of his going out last night to bring that drunken old William home! (If it were not for Captain McRoss, I would have discharged the dissipated creature long ago.) And then, when you all three came in out of that bitter storm, to think of my nephew being so foolish as to refuse a glass of rum. I'm glad *you* went, Sam, for, Hiram could not have got old Billy home alone. Afterwards, instead of warming himself, he actually went out for snow and rubbed that old wretch's hands and feet to draw the frost out! He would have scorned to do so, a year ago! But, to be silly enough to sign the Pledge—just think of it! Well, I'll coax him to break it!"

"You had better not, ma'am. The curse of Heaven will be upon you, if you do!"

"You Methodist! *Our* parson takes liquor and likes it, well. And, so do *you*!"

"*I've* not taken the Pledge, ma'am."

"I should hope not. Well, I am still more provoked because my nephew has given up all intention of farming; and, the only reason he can give, is the ridiculous one that 'he can't leave Mr. Grant!' It is dreadfully annoying."

That night, as they gathered around the fireside, Sam Wilkins observed, "It's my belief that Hiram likes the head-teacher more than anyone else."

"That is not true," retorted old Billy; "now, is it, young master?"

"It is scarcely true, sir," replied Hiram, gravely, "for, of course, I love my Saviour better than Mr. Grant."

There was a dead silence. They were all surprised, for Hiram had not spoken of his faith before. Then William caught sight of the palm of one of the lad's hands, which he had hitherto concealed as much as possible, and asked, "How did you hurt yourself so badly?"

Hiram's face flushed deeply as he answered, Mr. "Grant whipped me."

The old man looked bitterly indignant, and Miss Morris, greatly surprised, but Sam laughed heartily and clapped his hands for joy, as he said, " Good for *you*, young boss.

" *Now* you can't brag, as you always used to, that no one dared to touch you, and all such stuff. Oh, dear, I am right glad that the master had sense enough to use the rod, even though you are nearly twenty years old. I hope he made you cry."

" You ought to be ashamed of yourself, Sam," said William ; " a fine Methodist, aren't you ?" Then, half to himself, " It was *too bad* of Mr. Grant."

"Indeed it wasn't, sir," replied Hiram, earnestly. " I deserved flogging, and it was the kindest thing the Principal could do for me."

Sam laughed, and wondered greatly what had come over the " young boss." Before he had recovered from his astonishment, Hiram began to urge the old man to sign the Pledge. William said he could not keep it if he did, for the sight of beer and cider on the table every day would overcome him. Then Hiram earnestly entreated his aunt to banish liquor during meal-times, but she scornfully refused.

" I will sign if Sam does," said William, " for two can stand easier than one."

Hiram turned to Wilkins and begged for his signature. " I will take the Pledge," answered the Methodist, " if you can prove from the Bible that we should not drink liquor."

" I can't," said Hiram, " but Giovanni could. Oh, I wish he was here! I have not read those dry Temperance books, but only some stories. However, the Bible tells us to love one another, therefore you might sign for William's sake, Sam."

"No, I'll not do it, so you need not ask me."

"Is that Giovanni more healthy than he used to be? He should drink lots of beer," said Miss Morris,

• "I would rather see him in his grave," replied Hiram, hotly.

Laughs and bantering remarks followed, so that McRoss had great difficulty in keeping his temper.

A day or two passed—gloomy ones for Hiram, who was longing for a sight of Mr. Grant—and then came Christmas Eve. Sam called at the Post Office, and on his return after dark, handed Hiram a small packet. The lad recognised the writing at once as that of the Principal, and eagerly opened his treasure. It proved to be a large and beautiful gold locket, which, when unclasped, showed a very fine portrait of Mr. Grant on one side, and on the other a lock of his jet-black hair. Hiram kissed first one side and then the other, and burst out crying. Poor old William was distressed, for he never remembered seeing the "young master" shed a tear since the latter was a child. Miss Morris and Sam were greatly surprised; but the former, who was an ambitious person, now resolved to say no more against her nephew's going back to Roseville.

When the lad had recovered himself, Miss Morris inquired "how he found out that the Principal was so fond of him?"

"It is mostly too good to tell you," answered Hiram, his cheeks flushing deeply, "but I may safely mention this—Mr. Grant says he is my father."

Miss Morris almost started out of her chair. "Your father! Is he going to adopt you?"

"No, ma'am, I hope not. If he were poor, instead of rich, I would like him to adopt me *then*, and I would work for him; but as he is so wealthy, I prefer to remain as I am."

"You foolish lad—if you take care he will probably adopt you, and leave you a large part of his property when he dies."

Hiram's face burned with indignation. "How dare you say so, aunt? I——"

"Come, come, my nephew," interrupted Miss Morris. "I always saw that you were taking after your father and mother in this particular. They were both lamentably deficient in the love of money; Captain McRoss is so still, and Lily would have been just the same, had she lived. Happily, *I* am altogether different."

"I hope that Mr. Reed is well off then," observed Hiram, scornfully.

"He has at least as much property as myself, or I would never marry him," said the old maid. She then continued, earnestly, "Now, my nephew, do listen to me. When Mr. Grant is *dead* he won't need his money; *you* might as well have it as anyone else."

It is impossible to describe the anger and grief of Hiram McRoss. When he could speak, he said warmly,

"Never! *Never!* I hope and pray that I may not live a day longer than Mr. Grant; but, that we may die together."

"Hiram, Hiram, how can you be so wicked? Surely you do not mean *that!*"

"I *do* mean it, Aunt; and pray for it every day of my life! God willing, my prayer will be answered."

"How old is the Principal?" asked Sam.

"He is forty years old."

"Forty!" echoed Wilkins, "and you are not twenty! What are you thinking about, young boss? Do you want to throw away your life? Why, what a fool you are!"

"Not at all," replied Hiram, calmly. Then, opening the locket, he looked lovingly, oh, so lovingly, at the portrait, and said, with a happy smile, "My Saviour is very good, I think He will let me die with Mr. Grant."

Miss Morris relapsed into a sullen silence; and Sam Wilkins handed a letter to Hiram, who received it joyfully, though his lips quivered. He went off to his own room, to read it, first bidding them all "good night."

Then Miss Morris opened her mouth. "My foolish nephew won't be adopted, just because Mr. Grant doesn't happen to be a poor man! How very absurd! But, it's just like Hiram—who was always proud and independent!"

Sam observed gravely, "The young boss will soon give his teacher to understand that he would rather be excused from accepting any of his wealth—and, that worthy could not well even offer it, then ; unless, indeed, he wished to offend his so called *son !* Oh, dear ! If *I* had only Hiram's good chance of a fortune, which he is so madly throwing away by that prayer ! "

" Do you think that it will ever be answered ? "

" Think ! " echoed Sam, who considered himself a good Methodist, " I wouldn't like to try it ! Why should it not be answered ? If Mr. Grant dies, I would be very unwilling to stand in Hiram's shoes—that's a sure case."

" I never felt so provoked with anyone, in my life ! " declared Miss Morris.

" You need not, ma'am," said old Billy, and his voice trembled, " the young master is turning out splendidly, and will be a credit to us all ! "

" He *has* improved, certainly," replied Sam, " but, it is silly to throw away such a chance. The gold of the head-teacher has no charms for the young boss, it might as well be at the bottom of the sea, as far as *he* is concerned. And this, too, when he could so easily have enough of it and to spare. Oh, dear, if ever there was a perfect fool, it is Hiram McRoss ! "

In the meantime, the lad was reading his letter. It concluded with these words,

" I start to-day, for the ' other side.' My native State is ' glorious old Massachusetts,' and I long to set foot on her soil again. Take care of yourself, my boy, and remember your pledge. May God bless you, my darling young McRoss.

" Your affectionate father,
" GEORGE GORDON GRANT."

Hiram had a good cry over his letter, but, no one witnessed it. The next morning, at breakfast, Miss Morris " hoped that her nephew had come to a more sensible conclusion, about the money of the head-teacher."

"I cannot do better than tell Mr. Grant the whole thing!" gravely replied McRoss.

Miss Morris looked astounded. For once, she lost her temper entirely, and angrily exclaimed, " Hiram, you fool —as sure as ever you do that, you will never get a cent of Mr. Grant's money!"

"I don't think there would be much danger of it, myself," was the calm reply.

"Oh, young boss, you had better not!"

"Aunt's base proposal was more hateful to me than you have any idea of, Sam," answered Hiram, bitterly. Then, in a lower, softer voice, he added, " Why should I not tell what troubled me to *my father?*"

"I am *glad* he is so fond of you," said William.

"Let us drop the subject," rejoined Miss Morris.

From that time there was little peace for Hiram until the close of the holidays. Sam continually teased him, sometimes about his Pledge, sometimes about his "disgraceful flogging," and Mr. Grant's *kindness* in inflicting the same! Again Hiram's crying-fit would be used as a source of annoyance—and, everything else that the mind of the thoughtless Wilkins could lay hold of, Miss Morris joined in, from sheer spite, and openly urged him to break his Pledge, as well. Old Billy was an exception, he always took Hiram's part with warmth. McRoss looked to Him who is 'mighty to save,' and, he did not look in vain. To his own surprise, he succeeded in keeping both his Pledge and his temper, and thanked God, when the time came, for going back to Roseville Seminary.

CHAPTER VII.

"TEMPERANCE FOREVER."

"HOW very provoking," said Mr. Slow to himself. "Here are all those lads back again on my hands. To-morrow the classes commence, and Mr. Grant to go and send me word that he has just returned from the 'other side' and cannot leave Claytown for some days! A plague on the Yankees and their country, too! Happily, Hiram has a head-ache this evening; so, he will not care to give me much trouble."

The next morning at breakfast, Mr. Slow observed, "You are not eating anything, McRoss, and look so flushed. Does your head ache still?"

"Yes, sir; very badly. I foolishly exposed myself to infection at Oakville; but did not think of danger until this morning. It is, doubtless, the scarlet fever; and I must go home after breakfast."

"Go home!" echoed the astonished Mr. Slow.

E

"You don't suppose, sir, that I shall stay here and give the fever to Mr. Grant!" answered Hiram, indignantly.

"I verily believe that your first and last thought is about the head-teacher!" snarled the assistant. "Is it possible that you don't know that he has had it long ago; when *I* was down with it myself?"

Giovanni saw that Hiram looked doubtful and therefore reiterated his uncle's words. The latter then inquired, "Were they old school-fellows that you were visiting, and are they getting better?"

"They were former school-mates, sir. Two of them are dead, and there is no hope of the third."

"You foolish fellow!" exclaimed Mr. Slow, his voice trembling with nervousness; "and you were actually going poking home, through the cold with scarlet fever, of such a malignant type, upon you! What chance would there have been of your recovery, do you think?"

"Not much," replied Hiram, gravely; "but Mr. Grant's life is exceedingly precious, and mine is not."

"My superior will never forgive me if I allow you to go home."

"As the Principal has had it, I would rather stay here, because ——" and McRoss stopped abruptly.

"Go on," said Mr. Slow, anxiously.

"Because," continued Hiram, calmly, "if it comes to the worst, I would like to die in Mr. Grant's arms."

The assistant's usually cross face worked with emotion; at length he said huskily, "Go and put yourself to bed, and I will send John off at once for the doctor." Which he did, while McRoss gladly obeyed Mr. Slow's order.

In due time the medical man arrived, and pronounced it to be a decided case of scarlet fever—not, indeed, likely to prove dangerous, unless cold were taken; but serious enough to tax the vital powers of the patient considerably. Mr. Slow felt much relieved. The physician mixed some medicines and was just giving directions about their use, when Giovanni came in. Dr. Mays turned, with a scowl, to the intruder, who simply bowed and walked up to the table, where the bottles stood.

"It will be necessary for my patient to take liquor —"

"*It won't!*" fiercely interrupted Giovanni. "Uncle has promised to let *me* give him his medicines; and you need not order rum, brandy, or any kindred abomination; for I will never give him a drop; no, not to save his life!"

"You wicked scamp!" exclaimed the angry doctor.

"It makes no difference," said Mr. Slow, mildly, "for *I* have taken the Pledge, and do not care to give liquor to anybody, sick or well. My nephew has actually frightened me out of it."

"My patient *must* have brandy," said the doctor emphatically. "I will bring some this afternoon, and administer it myself."

"You may save yourself the trouble, sir; for I won't take it," said Hiram McRoss.

"You don't know what is for your own good," answered the physician. "I will bring some when I call, this afternoon." And he went out into the hall, followed by Mr. Slow.

"Oh, Giovanni," said Hiram, "you don't know how I

was tempted to break my Pledge, in the holidays. I never thought that I was so passionately fond of liquor, before. I will not take brandy if it be possible to help it; but, that doctor may force me. As sure as ever I taste the stuff again, all is over with me ; and I shall die a drunkard after all !"

"*Never*, McRoss ; " said Giovanni, earnestly. " You have given yourself to God, have done all in your power to resist temptation ; and, do you suppose that *He* will coolly allow you to be overcome, in your hour of weakness ? No, indeed, God takes better care of His children than that ! There is no drunkard's grave for *you* ! Do not be troubled, McRoss ; I will stay here and the doctor shall not give you a drop of liquor ;" and the boy raised his right hand, as he spoke, with a motion that said how gladly he would sweep every bottle of the poison from the earth.

The look of despair faded from Hiram's face ; and he gazed at the little, outstretched hand. It *was* little and thin and white.

" Promise me that you will not let the doctor give me a drop of liquor, until Mr. Grant comes back. It will be all right, then."

" I promise you," said Giovanni, calmly.

McRoss looked at the small, slight figure before him.

" I *wish* there was some strength in the arm you raised just now," he said.

" There *is* strength in it," replied Giovanni Somerville, " because it is nerved by the power of the Lord of Hosts!"

Hiram could not help smiling, though he felt miserably ill. "You are a queer boy, Giovanni; I'm satisfied now. God works by *means*."

When the time came, the doctor was as good, or rather, as *bad* as his word. He placed a bottle of brandy on the table and also one of port wine; both of which, he declared, would work like a charm. Giovanni was in the room, as pale as usual, but he did not open his mouth. The doctor sat down beside Hiram; and, finding that he was burning with fever, strongly recommended that his patient should be sponged all over, every two hours or so. McRoss laughed bitterly; and indignantly declared that that not one of them should touch him; no, not to wash his face! The physician assured Hiram that it would make him feel much easier; and urged Mr. Slow to insist upon it.

"Oh, dear," answered the assistant, "speak to *him*, not to *me*. Why, he will not let us comb his tangled hair, or wash his hands; and, he is too ill to do it for himself. Speak to *him* and bring him to reason, *if you can!* Such a proud, independent fellow, I never saw in my life. I always thought that Mr. Grant, with his Yankee notions was bad enough; but, Hiram McRoss beats me out and out!"

Both doctor and patient had forgotten, for the time being, all about the brandy. The former, accordingly, used all his arts of persuasion to induce the troublesome Hiram to submit to be sponged—the assistant joining in. Meanwhile Giovanni removed the bottles of liquor to the window-sill. A moment after, the window was thrown open; and, the lads in the school-yard, heard their comrade's clear, ringing voice yell out, "Hurrah, boys! *Clear the track!*" Looking up, they saw Giovanni leaning out of the window, with a bottle in each hand. He immediately dashed them to the ground, where they broke into numerous pieces.

The doctor started up. "You young rascal!" he exclaimed, "I'll pay you for that!" and he was going to give Giovanni a good shaking—if nothing worse.

"Don't, *don't*," said Mr. Slow, anxiously. "You will excite your patient; and, if anything goes wrong with Mr. Grant's favourite scholar, you will *never* have occasion to make another visit here, sir, I assure you!"

Dr. Mays immediately calmed down, or pretended to do so; for, during the last ten years, the practice he had derived from Roseville Seminary was considerable. So he said, "My patient is a favourite with the head-master, is he? What a pity that that gentleman is not here himself."

"Oh, it is indeed! I shall be truly thankful when he returns," remarked poor Mr. Slow.

"Don't trouble about me, sir," said Hiram, wearily, "the fever must take its own time. Oh, I wish that my head would not ache so," and, he tossed uneasily on his pillow.

"My good lad," said the doctor, coaxingly, "let your companion bathe your head."

"I *won't*," growled Hiram McRoss.

"Dear, dear, said the perplexed assistant, "what *is* to be done? The Principal is the only one who can manage him, and *he* is away."

"Continue the mixtures, and telegraph for Mr. Grant," said the doctor, abruptly, as he arose and left the room. Mr. Slow followed him, and sent the man-servant, John Haye, off at once, with the message. When he returned to the sick room, Hiram complained more and more of his head. Mr. Slow got extremely anxious; for the doctor had told him, that if nothing could be done, the lad would soon be delirious. "And in that case," thought the alarmed assistant, "McRoss might get up and go out in the cold, as others have done when light-headed. *I* am getting old and could not prevent him. No doctor in the world could save him after *that!*" Mr. Slow communicated his fears to his nephew, who immediately soaked a small towel in cold snow water, and quickly wringing it out, he gave it to Hiram, saying, "Put this on your forehead, McRoss."

The lad did so, and exclaimed, "Oh, that feels so nice!"

The following morning, about nine o'clock, the doctor came again. He at once asked, "Has the Principal returned?"

"Oh, no," answered Mr. Slow, "he has to come partly by train, and partly by stage—he could not get home before to-night."

"Have you brought any liquor, sir?"

"Certainly not. Hiram, I don't want any more of the delightful stuff wasted. When the Principal comes, however, I shall recommend him to dose you well with it. Of course, Giovanni's *valuable* services will then be no longer required."

" Very good, sir," replied Giovanni. " You may recommend it as much as you choose; and on Mr. Grant's head will be the shame and the guilt, if he give a single drop out of *the devil's cup* to Hiram McRoss !"

The doctor's cheeks flushed angrily. " This is no place to quarrel with that little temperance fanatic," he remarked, " so we will let it pass." He then turned to his patient and the sight moved him to pity. " My poor fellow," he said, " you are very foolish to be so touchy, why, that nice curly hair is dreadfully tangled, and—"

" There is no wonder," put in Mr. Slow, " for Giovanni says that he tossed about all night."

" Has your face been washed or your hands, since you were sick ?"

" No, sir . I would not let them do it."

" How miserable you must feel !"

" *So I do*," wearily replied McRoss.

Just then, John knocked at the door and said, " Mr. Grant's here; he hired a conveyance and travelled night and day." A moment more and the Principal entered. To the amazement of the doctor, he advanced immediately to the bed-side and kissed Hiram again and again.

" My dear boy," he said angrily, " how wretchedly they have neglected you."

" It was my own fault, sir," replied Hiram, bursting into tears of joy at having the Principal back. Even then he had enough of the old pride or independence, or *both*, to make him hide his face on Mr. Grant's breast, so that the others should not see him cry. The master clasped his arms around Hiram and drew up the bed-clothes over his shoulders to prevent any danger of cold.

"How you have excited him," exclaimed the doctor uneasily, as he heard Hiram sob.

"It's all right now," said Giovanni.

"You must need sleep, sir," remarked Mr. Slow, "your room is warm and comfortable."

"Thank you, I'm not sleepy," returned the Principal. So saying, he sent them all downstairs for a while, and then made Hiram look up and wiped his tears away. "Don't cry, my precious young McRoss," he said tenderly, as he kissed the fever-flushed face over and over again. Wrapping Hiram in blankets, Mr. Grant carried him into his own room, which was larger, airy and beautifully furnished. The lad protested against being put in the master's bed and inquired, "where are *you* going to sleep, sir?"

"Oh, on the lounge, which I will draw close beside you, so that you can wake me when necessary," replied the gentleman, lightly.

Soon the doctor and Mr. Slow were summoned upstairs. Giovanni, white as a sheet, stole into the room unasked. Hiram looked much more comfortable; his hair was combed out and brushed off his forehead, and his face and hands were washed.

"Why, my patient, you will let the Principal do anything he chooses, he must have carried you in his arms like a baby! Whatever *is* that gold thing which you keep squeezed in your hand? I noticed it, at my first visit, and it has apparently been there ever since! Will you let me see it?"

"Yes, sir," and Hiram smiled. He was leaning upon Mr. Grant, who was sitting upon the bedside.

The doctor took the locket from the boy's hand. He thought at first that it was a watch; but, speedily discovered his mistake. On opening it, and seeing Mr. Grant's likeness, the medical man laughed, and said, "well, Hiram, you *are* the master's pet, and no doubt feel proud of the honour. What a very fine picture this is."

"You may well say that," observed Mr. Slow.

"Oh, Mr. Grant, I can never thank you enough for it," said Hiram, as he received back his treasure.

"You foolish child," answered the Principal, smiling. He then took some lemons from his pocket, and said, "Giovanni, will you make a pitcher of lemonade for your school-fellow?"

"Oh, don't send him, sir," entreated Hiram. "He waited constantly on me yesterday; and sat up all night as well. I bothered him so much, too, wanting ice, coldwater, medicine or something, every few minutes. See, he is as white as a ghost—do send him to bed!"

"I'm glad that he has so much affection for his schoolmate," replied Mr. Grant.

Giovanni's pale cheeks flushed. "It wasn't *that*, sir, Of course, I like Hiram—but ——"

"But what?" asked the Principal.

"I was afraid, sir, that they would give him liquor; so, I always poured out his medicine myself. Last evening he got worse; and, uncle found some old rum, that the house-keeper had had stored away for years, in case of sickness. He said he would put a tablespoonful or so into Hiram's tea—that, as Hiram was slightly delirious he would not—perhaps—notice it. That was the reason I sat up all night—to prevent such a misfortune as his getting a single drop. He——"

"Now, Giovanni, what did you do with that rum? I am confident you took it from my hiding-place. *What did you do with it?*"

"I threw it out of the window, uncle, where the doctor's two bottles had gone before!—Mr. Grant," and the boys cheeks flushed, "you need not think that I deserve any credit for sitting up with Hiram—it was not for love of *him*, but for——" he stopped abruptly.

"For love of the Temperance Cause," said the Principal, smiling. He instantly became grave again, when he saw how exhausted Giovanni looked, and continued, "your nephew had better go to bed, Mr. Slow. *I* will take care that young McRoss has no liquor in his tea or any other way. Had you played such a trick on my boy, sir, you should not have stayed another day in the house. You may thank Giovanni for not being dismissed as it is."

"Indeed," said Mr. Slow, "I meant it for the best, being afraid that Hiram would die. Dr. Mays strongly recommended that liquor should be given."

"Certainly," remarked the physician, "it is my invariable custom. I prescribe wine, spirits or malt liquor for almost every disease in existence. People like these things—like to take them, except, when one comes across such a Temperance fool as Giovanni Somerville. *That*, thank Heaven, is very seldom."

"You ought to be ashamed of yourself, sir," exclaimed Hiram, angrily, "that boy is worth his weight in gold—the day may come, when you will be glad and proud to have him for your son-in-law!"

The doctor looked astounded—he was too much surprised to speak—and Hiram went on: "That little daughter of yours is just Giovanni's age—you must have noticed the loving glances which she casts at him in church——"

Hiram stopped abruptly, for Giovanni burst into such a merry laugh, that Mr. Grant could hardly keep his countenance straight, and Mr. Slow did not try. As soon as he got his mirth in check, the lad observed, "You must be mistaken, Hiram. There is nothing in me to attract her attention.—— But, Shuter sits in the same pew, and he is so good-looking that——"

"It's not *him* at all," said Hiram impatiently—"you must know that it's yourself!"

"I never noticed that she looked at either of us," said Giovanni, who had regained his usual grave demeanour.

"I'm afraid that Hiram is partly right," groaned the doctor. "Oh, dear! I see now what Hattie meant by asking so much about Giovanni. To think of my own lovely little daughter, my only and idolized child, falling in love with such a Temperance fool,——"

"She shows her good sense," angrily retorted Hiram.

"Don't excite yourself," said the young teetotaler, calmly, "all the evil names they could call me, would not hurt me in the least."

"The judgment day will reveal *who* is the fool," said Mr. Grant, firmly. "And doctor, if you administer any kind of liquor to young McRoss—there is an end to your practice in the Seminary."

Forgetful of the patient, Giovanni clapped his hands and danced out of the room, singing, "Temperance forever!"

"That odious boy!" exclaimed the angry doctor. "Wouldn't I like to shake him! *Very sick*—isn't he? It looks like it, truly!"

CHAPTER VIII.

" FATHER AND SON."

THE physician was greatly surprised when he found that the Principal was going to take care of Hiram himself, and therefore repeated his orders to *him*. "I'll call in a couple of hours' time, because my patient needs other medicine, as you won't give him brandy. Don't forget the sponge-bath, *that* always affords relief." Then, beckoning Mr. Grant outside the door, he said gravely, "You were very foolish, sir, to touch your lips to that boy's face. *Never* kiss a fever-patient."

The master laughed and the doctor went his way. " It is no use speaking to the Principal, he is as self-willed as Hiram McRoss," said the physician to himself. " My warning went in at one ear and out at the other. Of course, if he had the fever again, he would probably die— came *very* near it the last time. I never had a patient that it was such a pleasure to attend—so good and gentle, though he suffered acutely. When told that he was not likely to recover, he smiled calmly and said, ' Then, I shall soon be with *my Saviour.*' He was so fit for Heaven that I felt certain he was going there. Oh, how differently Mr. Slow behaved—cross, peevish, hateful— though he was scarcely sick at all."

The assistant and his nephew were at once released from any further attendance on Hiram. John took up his station in the hall to assist his master when necessary, while Giovanni lay down on his bed to get a little rest. He looked at the horrid picture opposite, and thus addressed the demons, " ay, you may all grin as you choose, but God will not let you get Hiram McRoss !"

About fifteen minutes later, a terrific yell rang through the house.

"That's my nephew—he's in a fit," exclaimed Mr. Slow, as, shaking in every limb, he hurried up stairs. To his astonishment, he found Giovanni peacefully lying on his bed, but wide awake.

"What in the world is the matter?"

"Why, did I scream out, uncle?"

"Scream! I should think you did! I only hope that you have not frightened Hiram."

"Oh, I'm so sorry," said Giovanni, "but it cannot be helped. I got to sleep, uncle, and dreamed that those demons were tearing Dr. Mays in pieces. It was enough to make one squeal."

Hiram's nervousness was soon quieted when told of the cause of the shriek. The conversation with the physician had excited him, and his head ached dreadfully. The Principal laid his cool hand on the boy's forehead.

"Dear Mr. Grant, I am so glad you have come back," said Hiram, with tears in his eyes.

"My poor child," replied the master, tenderly, "I wish I could bear the pain for you."

"I'm glad you can't, sir. My head is worse now, because I got excited in talking to the doctor. It was a shame for him to speak of Giovanni as he did. Miss Hattie has more sense than her father. Oh, my head is all in a whirl."

"Let me bathe it, young McRoss, and quiet yourself if you *can*," he added, "or I fear that delirium will set in again."

When the pain of his head was a little relieved, Mr. Grant proceeded to give Hiram a sponge-bath. The lad would have violently resisted the assistant or the doctor, but he was passive in the hands of the Principal. That gentleman was as tender as though the big boy before him were an infant. When it was over, Hiram felt much easier, and earnestly thanked Mr. Grant for the trouble he had taken.

"It is no trouble, but a *pleasure* to do anything for *you*, young McRoss. Did I hurt you?"

"Oh, no sir," and Hiram smiled, "you could not hurt me, for you were so gentle." He then added in a lower, graver voice: "Mr. Grant, I have not said my prayers yesterday or to-day."

"My poor child," said the master, who well knew by experience how the lad felt, "I don't wonder you could not collect your thoughts. But the Lord Jesus prayed for you, young McRoss."

Hiram smiled. "Yes sir, I know He did. I prayed in my heart, of course, but just in detached sentences, for I I could not *think*, and neither can I *now*. Dear Mr. Grant, please tell me what to say."

The Principal immediately knelt down and took Hiram's hand in his, while he slowly uttered simple petitions, which the lad repeated after him. There was something which the master designedly omitted; but McRoss remembered it, and concluded by praying: "and if it be Thy will, please Lord Jesus, let me die with Mr. Grant."

The Principal arose, his eyes were full of tears, but he controlled his emotion, and gave Hiram a drink of lemonade.

As Dr. Mays neared his home, his thoughts turned to his daughter. "Now there's my darling Hattie—(oh that odious Giovanni—though I'm sure it isn't his fault—*he* doesn't care a snap for her—not he)! my poor little girl —a perfect idol she has been to me since her mother died —that is nine years ago now. Oh, my angel wife, I promised to follow you to Heaven, and to bring up your child for the Saviour; but alas! I am not doing either. Hattie's nurse is a good Methodist—quite a saintly woman—but Hattie herself isn't saintly, nor likely to be. She is the picture of her dear mother, but, unfortunately, has my headstrong, determined nature in a twofold degree; and I have let her do just as she pleased— why shouldn't I? She is *my only one*; and what a comfort the wilful, saucy, little lass has ever been to her lonely father! I always tell her about my patients, etc., for whom else have I to talk to, I'd like to know! It seemed to interest the girl to hear news of Roseville Seminary, especially of Giovanni. Why, it is long ago that I pointed him out to her in coming from church. And now—oh, I've no patience to think of it." Here Dr. Mays entered his house, and Hattie, a girl of fourteen, came flying down stairs as soon as she heard her father's step in the hall. Following her parent into the parlour, she drew a low ottoman close beside him and seated herself upon it. Leaning forward on his knees and looking up into his face, the girl said, " You are grave, papa; is Hiram McRoss going to die?"

"Oh, no; he is not any better yet, it cannot be expected; but, the Principal is with him now."

"Can *he* make him mind?"

F

"I presume so," replied the doctor, smiling, "but it was more than *I* could do." And he gave his daughter a full account of his visit, save, of course, that he did not mention anything concerning herself.

"Oh, papa, is Giovanni sick?"

"You seem very anxious about him, my girl!"

"Tell me, papa, *is* he?"

"No—no—only tired. And now, Miss Hattie, I really believe you are in love with him! Yes, you may well hang down your head and look ashamed."

Hattie sprang from her seat and proudly raised her head, shaking back her long brown curls. Her rosy cheeks were crimson; but, she spoke clearly and boldly, "It's nothing to be ashamed of! I *do* love Giovanni Somerville, and glory in it!"

The physician said not a word. He opened his arms to his little daughter, who immediately rushed into them, and, hiding her face on his shoulder, began to cry.

"Oh papa," sobbed the girl, "you have got me *everything* I wanted, all my life long—now, do please get me Giovanni!"

Poor Dr. Mays was nonplussed, as well he might be, at such an unreasonable request. So he said, "you're a foolish child, Hattie; and don't know what you are talking about. You have listened to my stories of the lads in the Seminary until you believe Giovanni to be a hero—and, to say the truth, he is a very common place little mortal, indeed! Now, if you could see him and talk to him for a while——"

"I wish you'd give me the chance, papa!"

"So I will, my girl, as soon as Hiram is better; and you will be speedily disenchanted."

"Oh, no, papa; don't set your mind on that! *I* have seen Giovanni at church, and have a very fair idea what he is like."

"Hattie, if it were one of the other lads, I would not mind; but the absurdity of your taking a fancy to that red hot little fanatic! It's too bad."

"I can't help it, papa—I didn't mean to, but it just came itself! Besides, why do you object to him? Didn't you tell me, long ago, that he was a Christian?"

"Yes."

"Don't you think so still?"

The doctor's conscience compelled him to answer emphatically, "*yes.*" He then added tartly, "what makes you so particular about that point; are you a Christian, yourself?"

Hattie replied in a whisper, "I've hoped so—lately—papa."

The physician was silent for some time. Then he said, "I'm not sorry for *that*, my little daughter; but, I *am* sorry that you care for that boy. He will never love you, child, *never*—nor, anyone else, either. He thinks of nothing, talks of nothing, cares for nothing, but the Temperance Cause."

"Papa, from what you say, Giovanni must be very strong in his likes and dislikes. He has a *heart*; and, if the Temperance Cause takes it up altogether, why, I'll try to push a little corner of the cause out!"

"You can't do it."

Hattie laughed. "It's not necessary, papa. I'm sure he has room for me, too!"

"Oh, my child, you are so young; *do* give up all thought of him!"

Hattie sprang off her father's lap in anger. "No—no, papa! If I cannot marry Giovanni Somerville, I will *never* marry at all," and she ran out of the parlour.

Dr. Mays, who knew the determined nature of his daughter, was shocked by her bold words. However, he did not forget duly to fulfil his promise of calling again at Roseville Seminary—two hours after his previous visit. John, who was stationed in the hall, upstairs, told the medical man to go in very quietly, which he did, and was astonished to see that the Principal, in his black broad-cloth dress, had lain down to set Hiram to sleep, and, in so doing, had set himself to sleep, too. Hiram was lying so happily at rest in Mr. Grant's arms, with his curly head on the master's bosom. The face of the Principal was beautiful in its expression of calm repose. The doctor muttered to himself "Father and son!" and, after a long gaze on them, quietly withdrew. Mr. Slow insisted on his remaining for dinner, to which he agreed and remarked, "Mr Grant is a plucky fellow! The idea of his sleeping so composedly with a fever-patient! It is very foolish to run such a risk; but he evidently thinks there is no danger. I never thought before that the head-teacher was such a fine-looking man!"

"*I* did!" and Mr. Slow laughed heartily.

As Giovanni did not make his appearance at the dinner-table, the physician inquired, "Where is your nephew?"

"Oh, he's asleep yet; don't trouble yourself about him."

An hour or more passed before Hiram awoke. After seeing him and giving directions, the physician took his departure. At the hall-door, he was confronted by Giovanni, who stood before him as pale as a statue, with a roll in one hand and a pen in the other.

"Will you be good enough to sign the Pledge, Dr. Mays?"

The medical man burst into a fit of laughter, at such an unseasonable attack; but as he had been most kindly entertained by Mr. Slow, he could not think of injuring that gentleman's nephew. Therefore, he merely pushed the boy aside, and was going off without deigning to reply.

"Dr. Mays, don't go yet—I want to speak to you."

"What about? Why, Giovanni, your face is flushed to the roots of your hair," exclaimed the physician, laughing.

The lad looked full into the doctor's eyes, as he said, "I am sorry, sir, that you were made uneasy by Hiram's nonsense. There is not the least occasion. I promise you that I will not attempt to influence Miss Hattie's affections in the slightest degree——without——" he stopped abruptly.

"Without my consent, you were going to say," said the medical man.

"I *was* going to say it, sir," replied the boy, coolly, "but it is quite unnecessary; for of course you would never consent to let your daughter marry a 'wicked scamp.'" And Giovanni turned on his heel and ran upstairs.

For a moment the doctor was bewildered; but the thought of Hattie made him call out, "Giovanni—Giovanni Somerville, come back—I want you."

The lad came down quicker than he went up, and eagerly inquired, "Are you going to sign the Pledge, Dr. Mays."

"No, you little idiot," almost screamed the physician, "I only wish to say a word or two." He then went on in a different tone, "You have acted very honourably in this matter about my daughter, Giovanni. Many, in your case, would have taken advantage of such a thing for purposes of spite. But you are mistaken; my little girl has been petted and spoiled all her life long, and I am not going to cross her now. As far as *I* am concerned, she is free to marry the man of her choice, when she is older, of course."

Giovanni laughed. "Do you actually mean, sir, that you will give *me* (a fanatic, a Temperance fool, an idiot, etc.) a chance among others of winning your darling?"

It was the physician's turn to redden. He replied, "Yes; but mind this, when you see Hattie and talk to her, you may not like her in the least, and it is equally probable that she will not care two straws for you. But should it be otherwise, my lad, *all right.*"

The bell rang. School was called very late that afternoon, but Mr. Slow had had other things to attend to. Giovanni smiled and said, "Thank you, Dr. Mays," and then immediately entered the school-room, the door of which was only a few feet from the place where the doctor and he had been standing. To the boy's astonishment, Shuter was there; he had evidently been listening to every word.

Nothing was said at the time; but at the tea-table, Aleck, for a joke, repeated the conversation between the doctor and Giovanni in full. The latter was indignant, and declared that Shuter had acted in a dishonourable manner.

"So he has, my nephew. That's the way he recommends his religion."

"Shuter professes to be a Christian," said Tom. "I hope you are proud of your convert, Archie."

Campbell coloured. "You should not expect Christians to be perfect, Tom—the best of them have their infirmities and sins, too."

Shuter's face flushed. "I only did it for play," he said. "Was it wrong, Archie?"

"I'm afraid so, because you would not like Giovanni to do so to you. But I do not wish to judge, Aleck, for I often do wrong things myself."

"I never see them, then," snarled Mr. Slow, with whom Campbell was a favourite.

"Well, Giovanni, I envy you," said Shuter. "That girl is a lovely little creature."

"Be silent, all of you," growled the assistant.

At times, when Hiram felt a little easier, he told Mr. Grant about the first day of his illness, how afraid he was that the doctor would force him to take liquor, of the dreadful consequences that would follow, of his conversation with his young temperance schoolmate, of Giovanni's calmness, and his promise; and of how *God* enabled him to keep that promise to the letter.

"I owe a debt of gratitude to that boy," said the Principal, and his voice trembled as he thought how near the precipice his beloved " young McRoss " had stood. Could he have seen Hiram's own father at that moment as he lay raving in the cabin of the " Sea Bird," held down on his berth by three sailors, the Principal would have felt more thankful still that Giovanni had prevented the son of Captain McRoss from getting another drop of liquor.

At length the crisis was passed. The fever had spent its strength, leaving Hiram irritable, nervous, and weak as a child. The slightest thing would bring the tears to his eyes now, and he wondered if he would ever feel like himself again. Well for *him* that Mr. Grant was so patient and kind.

" You *must* take this medicine, young McRoss."

" I won't," and the spoon was upset.

A minute or two more and the master was offering another spoonful, which Hiram immediately spilled as before.

" You *can't* make me take it."

" You foolish child," said the master, sadly, " nothing would be easier than to *make* you mind me now. It is necessary for you to take that medicine, young McRoss; indeed it is entirely for your own good. Why are you so naughty?"

No answer.

"Won't you take it to please me, child?"

"No, I won't," was the cross reply.

For the third time the master stood by the lad's bedside, but now he held a leather strap. Taking one of Hiram's hands he began to whip him, without saying a word. As the Principal expected, the lad cried at the first stroke, but that made no difference. Of course, he was too weak to be punished severely, and it was not necessary. Mr. Grant would not have injured him on any account, but he took care that Hiram's hand, though not cut in the least, was red and sore before he laid it down. The boy, crying bitterly, immediately gave him the other hand, which was treated in like manner. Then, without waiting to ask if his chastisement had had the desired effect, Mr. Grant put his arms around "young McRoss" and kissed him. After a few minutes the medicine was taken without a word of complaint, but Hiram did not stop crying.

"What is the matter with you, child? Do you feel any worse?" asked the Principal in an anxious tone.

"Oh, no, sir, it is not that."

"What then—won't you tell me?"

"You don't love me now as you did before, Mr. Grant, do you?" asked the boy, with a fresh burst of sorrow.

The master's eyes filled with tears; his feelings were

deeply wounded, for Hiram was more than all the world to him. "Young McRoss," he replied, in a broken voice, "I had far rather you had boxed my ears than said that."

Hiram looked up in astonishment at such words from the dignified head-master of Roseville Seminary.

"Did you doubt my love because I whipped you when you were sick, child? It was to do you good, for you would not mind me without. You have hurt *me* far more than I hurt *you;*" and the tears, which had filled Mr. Grant's eyes at the boy's question, now rolled slowly down his cheeks; tears which the proud head-master would have let no one in the world but Hiram see.

"Don't cry, dear Mr. Grant," entreated the lad, who was in deep distress at the sorrow he had unintentionally caused. "Oh, I am so sorry I hurt you! That medicine is not nasty; it was from sheer hatefulness that I would not take it, but you were so kind and patient, and, even though forced to whip me, you were not in the least cross. Oh, sir, if you *had* got set against me it would have been all my own fault!"

"Child," said the Principal, hastily brushing his sleeve across his face, "I wish I could make you understand how I love you, *then* you would not be troubled with such thoughts;" and, as he leaned over to kiss Hiram, a tear fell on the boy's cheek.

With a sob he hid his face on the master's breast, saying: "Dear Mr. Grant, I *know* you love me as well as ever, and, oh, indeed, I love *you!*"

The tears of the Principal flowed fast as he said in

such tones of passionate love that Hiram remembered them to the day of his death, " My child, my little pet, my baby—I think it would kill me if God should take you away."

" I don't think He will, sir," was answered in a low, soothing tone, " Jesus is very merciful. I feel almost sure that He will let us die together. Oh, won't that be good ! "

" Yes, my darling," said the master, with a sob, " next to the joy of seeing my Saviour in heaven, will be the happiness of having *you* with me, young McRoss."

CHAPTER IX.

"HATTIE MAYS."

" NOW, Mr. Slow, do tell us how Hiram is ? " said George Thorne, that same day at dinner.

" Oh, he's as fretful and peevish as a baby cutting its teeth," answered the assistant. " I don't know when the Principal will be able to resume his duties again, for the lad is very weak. But *I* don't mind, for my salary is doubled while I teach alone ; and you must all acknowledge that I am bringing you on uncommonly well."

" Tell us something about Hiram, please."

"You seem remarkably fond of him, Thorne," snapped the assistant, "perhaps it will interest you to know that the eccentric Mr. Grant has been giving him a little fatherly correction this morning."

"The brute!" hotly exclaimed Thorne.

"Come, come, George, not too fast! I was just inside the room at recess, and noticed that a leather strap lay on the bed, while Hiram was crying in Mr. Grant's arms."

"It was a burning shame."

Mr. Slow laughed. "If you knew how cross and hateful that lad can be you would not wonder, though I believe he is sorry for it immediately afterwards."

"The Principal might have a little pity for him, then," observed Campbell, gravely.

"I guess he has a good deal, Archie. In fact I do not believe that that most patient head-master has spoken a cross word to the boy since he has been sick. But he makes him *mind*. Hiram gets petted enough, certainly; but he'll not get spoiled," and Mr. Slow laughed.

"What sort of a strap was it?"

"Now, Thorne, you need not feel uneasy. It was a leather strap, suitable for punishing a child. I don't doubt that Mr. Grant made Hiram smart, but I'm quite sure he would not injure him."

"It is most likely he deserved flogging," said Tom, with a shrug of his shoulders.

"Did you speak to him, sir," asked Thorne.

"Oh, no; nor to Mr. Grant, either. That gentleman

never condescended even to turn his head!" The reason *why* happily did not occur to the assistant's mind.

"I *hate* him!" said George Thorne; "he had no right to treat Hiram as if he were a naughty child."

The lads laughed heartily, and the assistant, too; at length the latter replied, "You have described McRoss accurately; he *is* a 'naughty child' and no mistake! Mr. Grant loves him as his own son—only, I verily believe, *far more dearly!* Of course, every teacher would not have used corporal punishment in such a case, but the head-master was always a peculiar man, *very* peculiar! Besides that, he knows Hiram better than any of us do."

"It is a wonder that Mr. Grant does not get tired of singing hymns," remarked Tom.

"He can probably soothe his big baby better in that way than any other," answered Mr. Slow. "What a memory the man has! It surprised me when I first watched him sing those long hymns without the ghost of a book in his hand. As for songs, he evidently does not know any, except those odious American things, 'Hail Columbia' and 'The Star Spangled Banner,' etc. I fairly detest them!"

"The Principal has a fine voice," observed Reynolds; "though, as a general thing, he makes precious little use of it—or that grand piano, either."

"He sings more in a week now than he did in a year before," remarked Tom.

"Yes," assented Mr. Slow. "It's a wonder to me that

he does not get weary with holding Hiram so much. He will sit and tell him stories by the hour together—true stories of the Revolutionary war. Of course it is the American view of the matter, making England wholly to blame. Hiram will be a regular Yankee by the time he gets down stairs again. You can't guess what Mr. Grant gave him on his birthday—can you?"

"No," said George Thorne. "When was it?"

"Only yesterday; now guess."

"Perhaps the Life of Washington."

"No—a lovely little silk banner of the Stars and Stripes, one-fourth the size of his own big one—and a beautiful Bible, bound in purple morocco."

"It is a good thing for Mr. Grant that Hiram ever came here," observed Archie.

"I think it's a good thing for Hiram," snapped Mr. Slow.

"Yes, sir, it's a good thing for both of them. The Principal deeply needed some one to love, though I don't think he knew it. He thinks all the world of that 'young McRoss.'"

"Yes," responded Thorne, bitterly, "and 'that young McRoss,' as you call him, thinks all the world of Mr. Grant."

"He has great reason to do so," growled the assistant; "are any of you lads senseless enough to believe that the head-master, wealthy and dignified as he is, would stoop to take the humble position of nurse to a sick, peevish boy if he did not love him as Mr. Grant never loved any one before? No! that he wouldn't, or my name is not Augustus Slow."

The boys laughed; but, there was not one of them who doubted the words of the assistant. That worthy concluded to pay a flying visit to Hiram's room before school was called. He did so, going just inside the door. The lad was evidently better—so the assistant said, and would soon be able to come down stairs again.

"1 hope so," replied Hiram, "for Mr. Grant must be tired of nursing me, especially when I am so cross," and the lad's pale cheek flushed.

"What makes you so?" laughed Mr. Slow,

"I don't know, sir," wearily answered Hiram; "but I do not feel in the least like myself."

"Perhaps my superior is cross to *you*; suggested Mr. Slow.

"Indeed, sir, he is not. Mr. Grant has never been anything but kind, all through my illness."

"He gave you a very kind and fatherly whipping, this morning, didn't he?"

"Yes, Mr. Slow," said the boy humbly, "it *was* a very kind and fatherly whipping. I know the other lads would not have had it, supposing they had been sick and would not obey, but Mr. Grant whipped me, because I was his son."

"Aren't you glad of it?" chuckled the assistant. "Now, as you are so candid, just let me ask whether your *father* did you any good by his loving correction?"

"Yes, sir; I would not mind him before."

"Don't you think it was very ungrateful?"

"Indeed it was, sir," replied Hiram, the tears coming into his eyes.

"That will do, my assistant, I will not allow him to be teased."

"Mr. Grant, please sing!"

"Very well, my child, what do you wish to hear?"

"I lay my sins on Jesus," said Hiram McRoss.

Mr. Grant sang:

> "I lay my sins on Jesus,
>   The spotless lamb of God;
>   He bears them all and frees us
>   From the accursed load.
>   I bring my guilt to Jesus,
>   To wash my crimson stains
>   White in His blood most precious
>   Till not a spot remains."

"That is more than enough of the hymn for *me*," muttered Mr. Slow to himself, as he stalked out of the room. "It shows what Hiram does with *his* sins; of course, I often tease him and pretend that he is only a make-believe; but, all the time, I know in my heart that he is a true Christian! How hard he fights against that passionate temper of his! He will *never* be rid of it as long as he lives—it's a part of his nature. But, I suppose it is *grace* that has enabled him to get it into something like control—of course, with all his care, it will obtain the upper hand of him sometimes; *that* must be expected. As for his being cross now, why, the foolish lad need not blame himself for that; because it is more the result of his illness than anything else. When *I* was recovering from the fever, I felt like biting people's heads off, had it been possible to do it; ding dong, ding dong—why, it's that Shuter at the school-bell!"

"Aleck, I've a good mind to warm your ears!"

"You had better not, Mr. Slow; the Principal says it is a very cruel punishment—ay, even a wicked one."

"Then, be off at once out of my way."

The doctor came late that afternoon. In passing through the hall, he encountered Giovanni, who again urged him to sign the Pledge, as was frequently the case.

"This is the *sixth* time that I have refused. I do wish that you would let me alone!"

"I'm not going to," briskly replied Giovanni, "and it makes no difference to me, whether you have refused six or sixty times."

"I wish I could discourage you! Did you have much trouble in getting your school-fellows to sign that precious document?"

"Nothing to speak of, sir; except in one case, when a comrade was somewhat obstinate."

"As *I* shall be;" snarled the doctor.

"He would not take the Pledge for nearly two years after coming to the Seminary. As far as I can remember I used to urge him every single day of each session—Sundays and all. Therefore you see it is vain to attempt to discourage me with only a sixth refusal."

The doctor looked excessively annoyed when he saw what was in store for him.

G

"What reason have you, sir, for not signing the Pledge ? At least tell me that," urged Giovanni.

The medical man hesitated, thought a moment, and replied, " alcohol is a good creature of God, and you know that the Bible says: 'Every creature of God is good and nothing to be refused.'"

"Do you dare to pretend, sir, that alcohol is a creature of God ? Did *He* make it ? No ; indeed. Alcohol is a substance that does not exist in nature. It is made by evil men, for evil purposes."

"Giovanni, you're a queer fellow; what good does all your Temperance do you ? "

"Now doctor, keep to the point, please. Suppose I grant your assertion for a moment that alcohol is a creature of God (mind you it is *not*, it's a creature of the devil—I'm *only* supposing it), does it follow that every good creature of God is to be used for food or drink ? "

" *Certainly ;* " was the reply.

" Then why not use arsenic for food ? "

" Oh, but arsenic is a poison."

" *So is alcohol.*"

The doctor could not deny it. He did not know what to reply, so he brusquely passed Giovanni and left the house. As he drove away he looked back towards Roseville Seminary and muttered " what a fine lot of Temperance fanatics that place will turn out, and all through the exertions of one plucky little mortal."

At length Hiram was able to come down stairs again and was warmly welcomed by his companions, especially

George Thorne. The latter had a headache at dinner and the assistant sent him to lie down in the dining-room as soon as the afternoon school commenced, for he saw that Thorne was too unwell to study.

"Hattie," said the doctor, "this is my last visit to Roseville Seminary for the present. Hiram will be with his companions to-day, though I have forbidden him to take any part in school exercises until he feels quite able to do so."

"You promised to take me, papa. I am very anxious to see Giovanni."

"You shall go, my child. But be prepared for a freezing reception from the Principal. He is a most eccentric man and has evidently a feeling akin to aversion for the whole female sex. Wouldn't I laugh if Hiram McRoss should take a fancy to you, but the head-master would never forgive me, never."

"Indeed, I hope he won't, papa, for I could not return it. Hiram McRoss is the big boy that always sits beside Mr. Grant in church, isn't he?"

"Yes, my girl; don't you like his looks?"

"Not so well as Giovanni's."

"*I* do, far better! What can you see in that Temperance lad, I wonder! He is small for his age, has a slight figure, very pale face, hazel hair, and large brown eyes. Hiram, on the contrary, is a good-looking boy—though not ——."

"Papa, Archie Campbell and George Thorne are somewhat alike—they are really handsome lads. Aleck is very pretty, but his features are too girlish."

The physician laughed. "He wears his flaxen curls so long that any one can see he is quite vain of them. Now, my dear, go and change your dress."

"Won't this one do, sir?"

"No, my girl, you must wear your sky-blue silk frock and white cashmere jacket."

"Do you wish me to take the head-teacher by storm, papa?"

Dr. Mays laughed. "I want him to treat you kindly, my daughter." The doating father did not know that he was going the wrong way to work.

The lads were studying as busily as usual when the school-room door opened and Dr. Mays walked in, closely pursued by Hattie. The lads gazed at the young lady. They saw that she was very pretty; her long golden-brown hair hung in thick curls around her face and far down her shoulders. Her eyes were as blue as her dress, and the roses in her cheeks especially attracted the notice of Shuter. Though fourteen years old, she was small for her age, and the short blue silk frock that scarcely reached to the tops of her high, kid boots, made her look younger than she really was.

Mr. Grant was much astonished and displeased. It was the first time that a girl visitor had entered his domains. The thought instantly flashed across his mind as he saw the gaily-dressed little beauty, "what if young McRoss takes a liking to her?"

The doctor introduced his daughter with all a father's pride, but Mr. Grant's reception of both was frigid in the extreme. The medical man was much hurt, and appreciated Mr. Slow's friendly greeting as never before. The assistant called his nephew, who immediately came forward.

"Hattie," said the doctor, "this is Giovanni Somerville. Giovanni this is my little daughter."

The girl eagerly stretched out her small white hand, and Giovanni grasped it cordially. At this moment, the Principal announced recess, and in the confusion, the assistant's nephew seized the girl by the hand and hurried her off to the dining-room. On hearing footsteps, Thorne arose and hastily concealed himself in a recess formed by a bow-window, drawing the curtains so as to hide him from view. He knew who the visitors were, having peeped into the hall while the doctor was taking off his overcoat.

"There's not an instant to lose, sit down, please;" and Giovanni half pushed the doctor's daughter into a chair and ran off.

When he returned, he said gravely, "Hattie, you've got to sign your name to this Pledge."

The girl took the pen which he put into her hand, and immediately wrote her name.

"Thank you," said Giovanni, heartily; "and now I want you to promise me, that you will *work* for the Temperance cause."

Hattie's blue eyes opened widely. "How can *I* work?" she asked.

"In more ways than I can tell you. Coax your father

to sign the Pledge, for *one* thing. Persuade him *never* to prescribe liquor for patients, under any circumstances whatsoever. Read Temperance stories to your old nurse while she is at needlework. Study up all about Total Abstinence and Prohibition; that will give you plenty to do, for there are so many phases of the question. Practise temperance hymns and songs, and then, sing them to your father. When a visitor asks for music, mind you always choose a Temperance song. Tease all your companions to sign the Pledge. Induce your father to start a 'Band of Hope' in Roseville. Do everything you can, and don't forget to *pray*, Hattie!"

"Oh, Giovanni, you're a *Christian*!"

"Yes—aren't *you*?"

"I hope so—but, oh dear, I do not love Christ enough."

"Neither do I; but for all that, I love Him, *my Captain*, above every one else."

"You're thinking of the Temperance army."

"Yes, Hattie," and the lad smiled. "*You* have joined it, mind you; for in this holy war, girls can be soldiers as well as boys. The cause is under God's protection. Every man, woman and child should fight for it—won't *you*? Remember, it is for our Captain, Hattie!"

"I know that, Giovanni," said the doctor's daughter, earnestly, "and I wish that I loved *your* Captain, *our* Saviour more!"

"Don't be shy of Him, Miss Hattie," said the boy. "Jesus is indeed your Saviour and your best Friend. Keep nothing from Him—tell Him everything."

"I don't do it," said the girl, in a low voice, "but I trusted Him with myself. Would not the little things of daily life, trouble Him?"

"Oh, no, Hattie," and the boy smiled. "I am sorry that you have missed so much comfort that you might have had. Don't let it be so in the future. Every joy or sorrow that comes to you, tell to *Him*."

"But, there are wrong things, Giovanni!"

"Yes, Hattie, that's very true. But, *tell them to Him*. The wrong deeds to be blotted out, the wrong plans to be set right. It is a happy thing that our Saviour-Captain is so forgiving!"

"Indeed it is!"

"Now, Miss Hattie, promise, please."

"Promise what?"

"To work—*to work until death for the Temperance Cause!*"

"I *promise*," gravely replied the girl.

"By the help of our Captain, Hattie!"

"Yes, Giovanni, of course, by the help of our Captain!" solemnly answered the doctor's little daughter.

George Thorne, just behind the curtains, heard every word. His conscience aroused again, began to prick him dreadfully.

Here the voice of the physician was heard loudly calling the name of his child. He had finished his business with the Principal, who was anything but cordial. The door of the dining-room opened, and Giovanni answered calmly, "Here is your daughter, sir; you had better follow her excellent example and sign the Pledge!"

The physician was speechless with astonishment. At last he said, "Hattie! Hattie! What possessed you to do it? You drank wine at your dinner to-day!"

"But I won't *to-morrow*, papa!"

"Oh, Giovanni," said the medical man, "you *are* a young scamp, and no mistake! I might have expected this—what an old fool I am! But, perhaps, it will turn out all right in the end. I hope so;" and the doctor hurried his daughter away.

In driving home he noticed that the girl looked grave. There was silence for some time. At last the physician remarked, "so you like Giovanni still, my dear?"

"Oh, yes, papa; more than ever."

"Very well, Hattie, it's all right;" said the medical man, with a sigh of resignation, "you might easily have done worse."

"Oh, but papa, he doesn't like *me!* I did not mean you to understand *that!*"

Dr. Mays laughed at the candour of his little daughter. "Did you expect him to fall in love with you at first sight?"

"No, papa; now don't make fun, please."

"I won't, my dear. You have got a fit of Giovanni's earnestness upon you by the look of your face."

"Papa, I've not been a good daughter to you;" said Hattie, sadly, "but I'll try to do better for the time to come."

"Whatever has come over you, child?" asked the astonished Dr. Mays.

"Giovanni made me *think*, papa; that is all."

At the tea-table, Mr. Slow observed, "I hope you did your best to make a favourable impression on the mind of Hattie."

"Indeed, uncle, I never thought of it."

"Oh, you stupid fellow, I thought you had more sense. I'll warrant you did your best to give her a favourable impression of the Temperance cause!"

"*Yes*, that he did," answered Thorne, with a laugh. "You look surprised, Giovanni; but you see I was hidden behind the curtains all the time and heard every word!"

"That was very dishonourable."

"I didn't mean any harm, Giovanni; but, you know I had a bad headache and was lying down in the dining-room. When I heard your footsteps coming, I just got up and slipped into the recess of that big window behind the curtains."

"Tell us all about the conversation," said James Bell, laughing.

"Not I, indeed," indignantly returned George. He then added, gravely, "Giovanni, there was not a word said on either side, that you might be afraid to let your Captain hear! Oh, how uneasy in conscience you two did make me feel!"

"I wish, Thorne," said McRoss earnestly, "that you would take your uneasy conscience to *Him*, who alone can quiet it."

"Oh, Hiram," exclaimed George, "I wish I was like *you!*"

The face of McRoss crimsoned. He had no time to reply, for Mr. Slow immediately snarled out, "*I* don't— Shuter and Hiram are a nice pair, truly they are! *If* they are Christians at all, *which I greatly doubt*, they are the most inconsistent ones that ever disgraced the name of Christ!"

The tears came into Hiram's eyes, and Shuter's face reddened. Mr. Grant was about to interpose sternly, when Aleck answered, " God knows whether we love Him or not! It is to *Him* that we must give account—and Mr. Slow, so must *you!* I wonder you like to live with God's curse upon you!"

The superstitious assistant shuddered. "You're a bad boy! How do you know it is upon me?"

"From the Bible, sir. ' If any man love not the Lord Jesus Christ, let him be Anathema Maranatha!'"

"Accursed at the coming of the Lord!" muttered Mr. Slow, "*fearful!*"

"It is indeed, my assistant," said the Principal gravely. "Young McRoss is safe in the arms of his Lord; and instead of attacking *him*, you had far better attend to the salvation of your *own* soul."

"So *I* think," seriously observed Thorne.

"*Ditto*, Mr. George," snarled the assistant.

As soon as supper was over, the lads went into the parlour to pay their school-fees, which should have been done at the first of the term, only the Principal was absent. When Giovanni's turn came, Mr. Grant said, "I shall never forget your kindness to young McRoss. Humanly speaking, everything depended on you, and you acted nobly. I shall not attempt to pay you, for the worth of such deeds cannot be estimated in money. One *day*, Giovanni, you shall have your reward! I believe you are collecting a Temperance Library, so *this* will buy you two or three larger volumes," and the master pushed a bright, gold eagle to the lad "and, thinking you might like to show your colours, I ordered this Temperance emblem."

"O, Mr. Grant, you're very kind," said Giovanni; "what a perfect beauty," and he surveyed the triangle with its central star and motto of "Love, Purity and Fidelity," most admiringly. It was an emblem of large size, exquisitely wrought out of pure gold. "But indeed, sir, I did not wish or expect anything. On the contrary, I thought you were vexed with me—that you *had* been vexed ever since I awakened you from your sound sleep in regard to Temperance. I had tried to arouse you by *gentle* means for over three years, but utterly failed. Hiram might have died a drunkard, had you slept much longer; therefore, it was better that you should be wakened. I beg your pardon that it was necessary to do it so roughly."

For the first time in his life, the master shook hands with Giovanni, saying, "I'll not give you my pardon; for you don't need it." Then the lad went back to his comrades and exhibited his prizes with joy. Hiram was the last scholar who went into the parlour. He took a chair beside the master, and noticed several little heaps of American gold lying on the table.

"Young McRoss," said Mr. Grant, "I do not wish to take any fee from *you*, and will return what I have received from you already," and he pushed the little shining heaps to the lad, saying, "That is for your first half-year—second—third—fourth—and this is the money which you have just handed to me now. Take it back, my boy; I don't want it from *you*."

The whole scene at his aunt's flashed upon Hiram's memory in an instant, and he replied, crossly and rudely, "I won't have it."

The flushed face of the Principal and his vexed look recalled the lad to a sense of his conduct, and, saying sorrowfully, "O, Mr. Grant, I didn't mean to vex you," he burst out crying, and covered his face with his hands.

The Principal was puzzled. He said, gravely, but not angrily, "Raise your head, young McRoss, and tell me why you answered so rudely. It was very unlike you."

Hiram obeyed, so far as to look up, but quickly bowed his head again, saying, "I'm *ashamed* to tell you, sir. It is about others, and has troubled me so much."

"Troubled you, young McRoss; then I have a perfect right to know all about it. Am I not your father?"

"Yes, sir;" and Hiram arose from his chair, seated himself on Mr. Grant's knee, and nestled close to his bosom.

The master clasped him tightly, and said, "I am sorry that you have got excited, for you are not well yet. Tell me the cause of your trouble, child."

Hiram raised his head, and, leaning it on his hands in

shame, told the whole story of the conversation at the farm-house fireside, his aunt's proposal, and the next morning's talk at breakfast. It had impressed itself on his memory most unpleasantly. At its conclusion, he was too much ashamed to look up. The Principal saw why Hiram had refused his money so bluntly, and, very naturally, thought more of him than ever. He saw, too, that the lad felt very badly, and was sorry for *that*. So he said, "You were not at all to blame, young McRoss. What have you to be ashamed of? It is well that your aunt is going to get a husband to her mind. Do not be surprised at her proposal, for, my dear child, *it is only the way of the world*. You have not seen as many of these things as *I* have. So, my darling, you would work for me if I were a poor man, but absolutely refuse to let me share my wealth with you. Is that fair?"

"Forgive me, Mr. Grant, please. I was very rude, but I want your love, and not your money."

"I have nothing to forgive," and the master's voice trembled. "Raise your head, my boy; you have no reason to feel ashamed. Poor child! I'm glad that you told me. Cast it from your thoughts—it need not trouble you now."

At this moment the assistant entered, and, seeing the gold, exclaimed, "How very beautiful!"

Hiram smiled. Drawing out the locket from his bosom, he said, "*This* is worth all the gold in the world to me!" and he kissed Mr. Grant's picture again and again.

The assistant laughed and sneeringly inquired, "Why don't you kiss *the original*, as he is close beside you?"

Hiram's face flushed and he hung down his head. The master, pitying his confusion, took off the attention of the assistant, by remarking, "I have just been offering these little heaps to young McRoss; but he will not touch a single coin!"

"How excessively foolish!" exclaimed Mr. Slow.

CHAPTER X.

"GIANT DESPAIR."

HIRAM'S health continued to improve; and, to his great joy, he soon felt like himself again. One day, the Principal bestowed a severe reproof on his highest Latin Class in general, which made some of the culprits feel ill-natured. Bell would not join his companions in play; and Hiram looked so fiery, that they let him alone.

"Where is Archie?" asked Ivon.

"He stayed in the school-room to study his lesson;" answered Shuter, "which is more than I would do, after Mr. Grant's lecture! It is queer what a hardening effect that creature's scolds have upon me. He has made his favorite Hiram, *cross*, this afternoon, and no mistake!"

At tea, Mr. Slow, who took every occasion to sneer at his scholars, snarled out, "did not your class do well, Shuter? I gave Hiram a 'piece of my mind' about it, this afternoon. Dear me; and yet, several of the lads, who failed so badly, pretend to be Christians."

"We don't *pretend*;" answered Shuter, "we *are* Christians."

"I'm not so sure of that;" grunted Mr. Slow, "James Bell was dreadfully sullen, while Hiram was as cross as a bear, at first, and then gloomy as an owl!"

McRoss angrily replied, "It was as much as I could do, to keep my hands off you, sir!"

"Then, it was *well* you controlled yourself," said Mr. Grant, sternly.

The assistant continued, "Both James Bell and Hiram profess to be Christians—Giovanni and Archie ditto. They all came in for a good scold and probably deserved it. I'm sure the first two did, at all events. And then, there's that Shuter! Another precious specimen of Christianity for you! *When* did he ever learn anything perfectly in his life?"

"Oh, lots of times!" said master Aleck, who was both able and willing to take his own part. "Depend upon it, Mr. Slow, if I were not a Christian, I would never learn anything at all, without being compelled. Oh, how I do detest lessons!"

"Detest *me*, you mean!" snapped the assistant.

"Why didn't you add 'and Mr. Grant too?'" coolly inquired Aleck.

"You incorrigible fellow!" growled Mr. Slow.

"You should not judge Christianity by the conduct of

its professors, sir," said Campbell, colouring. "Judge it from the Bible, from the life of Jesus Christ."

"Very true, Archie," remarked Shuter, gravely, "they ought not to take *us* for model Christians, any more than we take *them*, the Principal and his assistant, for model teachers!"

The naughty Latin class nearly all laughed, but the two gentlemen looked annoyed. They could not punish Shuter for so grave a remark, although it hit them hard.

"What do you say to *that*, Hiram?"

"*Mr. Grant* is a model teacher, Mr. Slow."

"And what am I?"

"*A model of peevishness!*"

The Principal sternly inquired, "Do you want another horse-whipping, young McRoss?"

"If you choose to give me one, sir."

"Isn't Hiram a model scholar?" sneered Mr. Slow.

The master hastily replied, "He has been more trouble to me, than any half-dozen of the others!"

The excited feelings of Hiram were stung to the quick. He replied in a tone, so hopeless, that even Mr. Slow was touched, "I know it, Mr. Grant; but, you can turn me away to-night, if you wish, and I will never, *never* trouble you any more!" Before they could answer, he was off to the school-room, while Archie gazed sorrowfully after him.

Half-an-hour later, the culprits were all seated around the table in the dining-room, for an hour's study, as a punishment for the missed lesson. The boys had been teasing Hiram worse than ever; and now he would not give attention to the task at all.

"You are not studying, McRoss," said the Principal, sternly.

"I don't intend to, sir."

"Oh, do learn it!" entreated Campbell.

McRoss immediately turned to the speaker, and saying passionately, "It's none of your business!" struck Archie such a savage blow that it cut open his cheek. The blood gushed out and the sight cooled Hiram's anger; but, he stood there, cold and indifferent. Mr. Slow was furious and demanded that the offender should be flogged at once; but Archie interceded so earnestly for Hiram, that the Principal could not refuse his request. So he said sternly, "Go up stairs, immediately, McRoss; and, if you are not in bed when I come (in half-an-hour's time), all Campbell's entreaties shall not save you from being well horse-whipped."

The lad took a lamp and went out. Archie quickly followed him and asked coaxingly, "Hiram, won't you do me a favour?"

"Yes, Archie, of course. I am sorry I hurt you."

"Thank you, please go to bed at once."

"I will before the master comes, as you wish it," answered McRoss, bitterly, "but, Archie, I would not mind being flogged, if it would do me any good. But it won't —*nothing will*. Oh, I wish I was dead;" and he brushed past his companion and ran up stairs.

Archie went back into the school-room with a face so

H

shocked that both teachers and scholars were surprised. Mr. Slow came and examined the wound. His hands shook as he removed the blood-stained handkerchief from the lad's cheek.

"Oh, Archie, you must have that cut sewn up; or it will leave a scar for life."

"I wouldn't mind a dozen scars," answered the boy, excitedly, "if only poor Hiram——" he stopped abruptly and burst into tears.

"Think of yourself, child, and not of that wretch," snarled Mr. Slow, "My superior will stitch this up nicely; and then, you will not be disfigured."

"I won't let Mr. Grant touch me!"

"My hands shake too much; I'm so nervous," replied poor, anxious Mr. Slow.

"I will not hurt you more than it is possible to help, Campbell," said the master.

"Won't you?" exclaimed the boy, bitterly, brushing away his tears, "when you could give poor Hiram such a brutal flogging as you did, I wonder *what* you wouldn't do to me, if you had a chance! No, no, sir; excuse me, please!"

The Principal coloured deeply. "Do as you choose," he coldly replied.

At this moment, Giovanni came up, with needle and thread. "I'll do it for you, Archie," he said, calmly.

Campbell turned to him at once, and the young Temperance advocate went through his task unflinchingly, which surprised the boys. *They* did not know that, when a mere child, Giovanni, with trembling hands, had sewn up a gash on the forehead of his own father, who had fallen and cut himself badly in a drunken spree.

"I did not think before that Mr. Grant was so *very* unpopular," observed the assistant. The lads laughed. "I guess *he* knew it," replied Francis Reynolds.

"I am quite as popular as I wish to be; *that* does not trouble me in the least," said the Principal, calmly.

"I don't doubt it," snarled Mr. Slow, "but did it never strike your acute Yankee mind that if the boys get set against you, they will be apt to think that the religion you profess is as cold and hard as yourself?"

Mr. Grant winced at the question, and his face flushed crimson. He did not wish to speak in his own defence. He knew that *the only one* who would take his part through everything was not by his side now. Hiram McRoss had been angrily sent off to his room, where he was having a hand-to-hand fight with Giant Despair.

The assistant saw the confusion of his superior, and sneeringly inquired: "Don't you wish that your favourite was here? *He* takes your part with a vengeance. Hiram McRoss evidently thinks you are an angel on earth—but the rest of us don't—*not we.*"

Mr. Grant looked still more confused, but he did not attempt to reply. Therefore the assistant resumed his attack. "Come, the lads will like to hear. Does my worthy superior wish us to consider his religion as cold and hard as himself?"

"The religion of Jesus is neither cold nor hard," said

the Principal, gravely, and he left the room. Archie followed him out, and put his hand on his arm. The Principal shook it off at once, but stood still.

"You are not going to scold Hiram, sir?"

"Why not?" was the cold inquiry.

"Because you will do very wrong," said Archie, in a tone of distress." He is desperate *now*, and has evidently given up in despair, for he wished that he was dead. Oh, Mr. Grant, what if Hiram's soul is lost after all."

The face of the Principal turned pale as marble at the dreadful thought. Then the blood slowly returned, as he recollected the difference between Archie's belief and his own. He replied gravely: "I am not a Methodist, Campbell. *That* is a point in which they are in error, for believers do not finally fall away. 'Once in Grace—always in Grace.' Their life is hid with Christ in God. My precious young McRoss is safe—so safe that he can never be lost. He is *saved*—eternally saved, through Jesus Christ our Lord."

"Amen," said Archie, earnestly. "Mr. Grant, it was through you that Hiram was converted. Now, do you suppose that the Christian life has been smooth sailing with him, as it has with yourself?"

"I'm afraid not," said the Principal, "and I have not helped him as I should have done."

"He needs it," said Archie, sadly, "for he is weary—weary of fighting. He never said a word about it to me, until now; but I can see how he struggles against his evil temper, every day of his life. Oh, what a bitter,

bitter conflict he will have. And then; when under great provocation he gets cross and angry (the boys say that Mr. Slow drove him almost wild this afternoon), he loses heart at once, and is altogether discouraged. *We* see how changed he is for the better; but he is blind to it himself. I am sure that he suffers more than we have any idea of, for I have watched him closely. O, Mr. Grant, you won't be cross with him, for he is just desperate as it is?"

"No, I won't," said the master, gravely. "I am glad that you spoke to me, Campbell. I feared that my boy would have a severe struggle with his hot temper, but did not anticipate this. I will do all for him that I can, but he is in better Hands than mine."

"Thank you, sir;" and Archie went back to his companions. A minute or two later, and the Principal entered his favourite's room, and while placing his lamp on the table, saw that Hiram's Bible was open at the fifty-first Psalm. Hiram himself was lying in bed, with his face buried in the pillows. The master sat down on the bed-side, and laid his hand on the boy's curly hair, saying, tenderly: "young McRoss." The lad raised his head. He had not been crying, but there was a cold, stony look about his face, which proved the truth of Archie's words.

"Don't, Mr. Grant, please;" and Hiram calmly pushed off the master's hand.

"My boy, you never did *that* before;" said the Principal, gently.

"You make it harder for me, than it need be, sir;" was

the gloomy answer. "I don't wish to stay here to trouble you any longer. It is surprising how you could have wasted your affections on one so utterly unworthy. There's Ivon, who will far more than fill my place. He is a dear little fellow, not much over ten years old; and you can adopt him, for he is an orphan, and will make you a good son. I have been nothing but a trouble to you from beginning to end; but it need not be so any longer. I have got nearly everything packed up; and shall be ready to start to-morrow. But—" he added bitterly, " I think you *might* have left me in peace, to-night!"

The Principal was surprised and grieved beyond measure. He said, " Young McRoss, a hundred Ivons could never fill *your* place in my heart! What are you thinking of? You have been more trouble to me than any half dozen of the others; but, that trouble you have repaid a thousand-fold. I confess that you would not think so, by the way I spoke down stairs. But, my boy, will you leave me because of a few harsh words spoken in haste?"

"O Mr. Grant, Ivon will fill my place far better than you think."

"He won't, child; and shall not have the chance. I never loved any one till *you* came here; you must know *that.*" He then added very sorrowfully, " I have passed my fortieth birthday, young McRoss; are you going to leave me as I begin to go down hill?"

Hiram was touched. "Dear Mr. Grant," he said, "I will *never* leave you, unless you wish it. But, oh, you *do* stand in your own light." He then added in a despairing tone, "However, if I *stay* here, even you cannot keep me from going all to the bad!"

"No," said the Principal, calmly, "I *cannot;* and, neither can I keep myself. But *that* does not trouble me in the least; for, there is One who will keep us both. I am not afraid to trust myself and you in His hands. Young McRoss, do you think that my confidence is misplaced?"

"No, sir;" was the firm answer, "not in regard to yourself; but, in *my* case, it is."

"Archie told me what you said to him. O young McRoss, how could you wish you were dead?"

"I *did* wish it, sir; for, I thought that both God and you had cast me off!"

"My boy," said the Principal, in a shocked tone, "you must not speak in such a way."

"It's nothing but the truth."

"I saw that your Bible was open. Were you reading the fifty-first Psalm?"

"I read the first verse or two; but, it was no use. I suppose, sir, you will be asking me, next, whether I said my prayers; so I'll just tell you at once that I didn't!"

Mr. Grant arose; and, taking Hiram's Bible, returned to his seat on the bedside, saying, "I'll read a chapter for you, young McRoss." He then turned to the account of the crucifixion as given by Luke; and, long before he had finished the story of the sufferings and love of Jesus, Hiram was crying like a child. The Principal was rejoiced that the stony coldness of his favourite had given way. There was more hope of comforting him now.

When the chapter was concluded, Mr. Grant took his handkerchief and wiped away Hiram's tears. "Young McRoss," he asked very gently, "are you going to give up your Saviour?"

"Not if I can *keep* Him, sir!" sobbed Hiram.

"Keep Him! You foolish child, *He* will keep *you*. When a baby is carried in its mother's arms, do you think it need be very anxious for fear it should not hold fast enough to its parent, and therefore be in danger of getting killed by a fall?"

"No, sir; the *mother* would hold *it*; and the baby would be a foolish little thing to be at all afraid."

"Very well, young McRoss; *you are just like that baby.*"

"Am I?" and Hiram smiled through his tears. "Will Christ hold me like that?"

"Yes, my darling, only far, *far* more safely. If He suffers you to stumble on your heavenward journey it is to try you, as He has so often tried His own; or as a punishment because you have neglected to look to Him."

Hiram replied in a low voice, "I thought He had given me up altogether, sir."

The tears came into Mr. Grant's eyes as he said, "Oh, no, young McRoss; you are too dear to the heart of your Saviour for that. You have no cause to fear, for *He* will never part with you,—will *never* give you up. Nothing shall separate you from His love. ' Because *He* lives, *you* shall live also,' according to His promise ; and as sure as the Lord Jesus is in heaven Himself, so surely will He bring you there too."

" Oh, Mr. Grant, you have comforted me so much! He will forgive me after all."

" Now, my boy, you had better say your prayers, at once."

" Yes, sir," and Hiram rose and did so.

When he was lying down again, the master said, " Tell me all about your trouble, young McRoss."

Hiram opened his heart to the Principal as he would have done to no one else on earth ; and lovingly did that gentleman cheer, advise, and help him.

" You are fighting bravely, my boy, and your crown will be a brighter one than as if you had no evil temper to overcome."

" Oh, Mr. Grant, do you think so ? But——"

" But what ? Tell me all, child."

Hiram raised himself up, and laid his head on the master's breast.

" *This* has troubled me more than anything else, sir. I am *worse* since becoming a Christian than I was before."

" Oh no, my boy ; you may *think* so, but that is all."

" Oh, but I *know* it," said Hiram, mournfully. " There are evils in my heart that I never dreamt of."

" Very likely ; but do you suppose they were not there before ?"

" Of course not ; I never knew anything of them."

" That might easily be, my child. God does not always

show young Christians much of the evil in their hearts; frequently *just enough* to make them feel themselves sinners, and *lost* without a Saviour. Having embraced that Saviour their spiritual education is begun, and God shows them the hidden evil of their hearts by degrees, as they are able to bear it. I do not say that this is the universal mode of God's dealings with His children, but it is very frequently the case. Hundreds have felt discouraged, like yourself, when they had no reason to do so. They have been walking for years in the heavenward path, and yet see more evil in their hearts than ever. I have felt it myself, young McRoss."

" You! O, Mr. Grant, did *you* feel discouraged?"

" No, my boy; for I knew the explanation of it." He then added in a lower voice, the blood rushing to his face as he spoke, " The increasing, *ever*-increasing, knowledge of my sinfulness is very humbling. It does me good, for it hurts my pride."

" I did not think that *you* were proud, Mr. Grant," said Hiram, in a low, sympathizing tone, as he clasped his arms around that gentleman.

" Has not my assistant told you so, twenty times over, young McRoss?"

" I scarcely believe anything he says," answered Hiram, indignantly.

" He was right enough there," said the Principal, sadly; " but I have no reason to be proud. We, none of us have. Did the increasing knowledge of your sinfulness discourage you very much, young McRoss?"

"Oh yes, sir. I have often felt wretched on account of it; but it is all so clear now. You are an angel of God to me."

Mr. Grant smiled. "And what are you to me, young McRoss? You are son, friend, and favourite scholar, all in one."

"And baby," suggested Hiram, with a laugh.

"Yes," said the Principal, "and *baby*. You are *God's* precious gift to me, young McRoss. I hope to keep you now, for you promised *never* to leave me unless I wished it."

"*And neither will I!* Do you suppose I have any one on earth as dear as you are, Mr. Grant? No, nor in heaven either—except my Saviour!" and Hiram nestled his curly head more closely to the master's bosom. The heart of the Principal was too full for words. He kissed the boy fervently, and rested his cheek on Hiram's dark hair. There was silence for a long while. Suddenly, the lad enquired, "Mr. Grant, are those unfortunate creatures at that Latin yet?"

The master laughed. "Probably they are. I forgot all about them; but it is time to send them off to bed," and Mr. Grant laid Hiram back on his pillow, and saying, "good night, my little pet;" he kissed him tenderly and left the room.

CHAPTER XI.

"THE RUMSELLER'S LAMENT."

"DR. MAYS, can't you give some substitute for port-wine. The Easter holidays are nearly here and I want to go home—I do, indeed!"

"Certainly, Tom, you wish to see your parents. Your pledge allows you to take liquor as a medicine, so why hesitate longer? Drink this nice glass of wine and continue to take it regularly—*then* you will feel strong enough to go home for vacation."

"Oh, dear, it's too bad. I hate to drink the stuff—but suppose I must, for father has promised me a gold watch this Easter!" and Tom drank off the wine.

"That's a good boy! Now, I must go or it will come recess-time, and that Giovanni—"

Alas for the doctor. The lads were leaving the school-room as he went down stairs. The young Temperance advocate instantly set upon him, and the medical man being determined to brave the matter out, said sarcastically, "I have just given a drink out of (what *you* call) *the devil's cup*, to Tom Harding!"

Giovanni turned paler than usual. He calmly asked, "Have you a good imagination, doctor?"

"Yes, I think so," was the amazed reply.

"Will you imagine what I ask of you?"

"Certainly, if I can," said the physician, who felt relieved that the lad had apparently forgotten that there *was* such a thing as Temperance.

"Thank you, sir. Now, please, close your eyes and imagine that you are standing before the great white throne, *God's* judgment bar, and that Tom Harding stands beside you and says, '*Dr. Mays, you made me a drunkard!*'"

The physician looked shocked. He had to comply, being a man of his word. So he closed his eyes and kept them closed far longer than was necessary. Poor Doctor Mays! For twenty-five years of his life he had recklessly ordered liquor—in many cases with direful effect; and the ghosts of his poor patients, long laid out of sight in drunkards' graves, now seemed to rise up before him. One, in especial, looked peculiarly terrible. It was Joseph Wilson, who received his *first* and *last* glasses of liquor from Dr. Mays. The first was a draught of wine, given to relieve the patient after a severe illness—the last was a tumbler of brandy and water, given four years afterwards, when the young man was dying of delirium tremens. The physician opened his eyes, and half-unconscious of Giovanni's presence, mournfully remarked, "If I *do* give up prescribing liquor now, what good will it be, for I have ruined so many?"

"You need not ruin any in the future, sir, and the past can be washed out."

"How, my lad?"

"By the blood of Jesus," said Giovanni.

"That is a comfort," said the troubled doctor, "now, I don't say that I will go so far as to sign the Pledge ; but, I *do* promise that I will be *very* careful how I prescribe another drop of liquor!" and he rushed upstairs and astonished Tom by telling him that he would send a substitute for the wine. Accordingly, Dr. Mays carried the bottle away with him. Harding improved rapidly and was able to mingle with his companions before vacation. Giovanni urged the physician to sign the Pledge, but in vain. When the medical man made his last visit to Tom, he invited Giovanni to spend the Easter holidays with Hattie and himself at Roseville.

"Thank you very much, Dr. Mays, but Hiram McRoss wants me to go home with him."

"You can divide your vacation, my lad, and give us each a share. Isn't Temperance work as good at Roseville, as elsewhere ?"

"Yes, sir. Your plan is a good one, and I will accept your kind offer with thanks. Tell Hattie—" he stopped abruptly.

"Tell Hattie what ?" asked the doctor, laughingly.

Giovanni coloured. "How *glad* I shall be to see her again."

"Very well," answered the physician, " we shall expect you," and he took his departure.

On the following Thursday, Hiram and Giovanni were in the stage on their way to Oakville. They were talking earnestly, notwithstanding the presence of a strange gentleman, who sat just opposite.

"What is the work you wish me to do ?"

"Why, to prevent Aunt Nelly from having wine at her wedding, to convince Mr. Sam that Temperance is taught in the Bible, to make him and William sign the Pledge, the latter is becoming a poor, old toper; but he will join the Teetotalers if Sam Wilkins will, too. Try your hand on Aunt Nell's husband-to-be, and draw him over to your side, etc., etc. Is that plenty of work for you, Giovanni?" and Hiram laughed.

"I dón't know, we can *never* do enough," was the grave reply. Seeing the gentleman opposite, smile, the young teetotaller drew out his pocket Pledge-book, with pen and ink, and eagerly asked him for his signature.

"I'm a wholesale liquor-dealer, Giovanni! There, I knew that you would look shocked," he continued with a half-laugh. "The traffic will never be put down— *never.* Even the Temperance fanatics say it will be a difficult task to undo the evil *we* are doing, for they declare that *all hell is with us.*"

"Much joy of your allies," replied Giovanni Somerville. "Let the rumsellers—backed by the devil and his angels, do their worst, they can *never* conquer, for *all Heaven is on our side.*"

The liquor-dealer smiled, he was more amused than offended by the boy's earnestness.

"It is no subject for mirth," said Giovanni, sorrowfully, "you are far too precious to be lost in such a wretched business as that."

"Precious!" echoed the gentleman, "there is no one *now,* who would say that of me except you."

"Pardon me, sir, you are mistaken. *Christ* thinks you precious, or He would never have died for you."

The liquor-dealer felt strangely moved. There was a choking sensation in his throat. He answered at last, huskily. "What do you wish me to do?"

"Sign the Pledge—pour out every drop of liquor, and give up the business for ever."

"Why, child, I have thousands of dollars embarked in the traffic!"

"Very well, sir; and what then?"

"How fearfully I should lose."

"No, sir; *you would not lose a cent!*"

The gentleman looked much surprised. "I don't understand," he said.

"I mean, that, if for Christ's sake, you give up that accursed business, He will not suffer you to be a loser. No, He has promised that you shall receive a hundred-fold, *now*, in this life—and, in the world to come, Life Everlasting."

The liquor-dealer was more affected than he cared to acknowledge. After a pause, he half-playfully remarked, "It is a pity, Giovanni, that you are not a minister."

"I hope to be a Temperance lecturer, sir."

"Indeed!" and the gentleman laughed. "Then I wish you success in your Cause."

"You, a rumseller!" said Giovanni, "and wish success to the Temperance Cause! Your *heart* cannot be in the business."

"It never *was*," muttered the man.

"Then, *do* give it up. You will rejoice that you did so, in the Judgment Day."

"Not yet," was the faint answer.

"What shall it profit a man, if he shall gain the whole world and lose his own soul?" solemnly repeated Giovanni.

The gentleman made no reply.

"Will it annoy you, sir, if I sing a Temperance song?"

"Oh, no; it will amuse me."

"I hope not," thought Giovanni. Then, saying calmly, "It is called the 'Rumseller's Lament,'" he commenced to sing the piece in a clear voice, so that every word could be distinguished. The liquor-dealer listened earnestly to the touching song. At the second verse, which is given below, he buried his face in his hands.

(2) "You've a crown, and a robe, and a palm, mother,
    And from toil and from care you are free;
    All the gold of this world I freely would give,
      If I could but share them with thee!

Cho.—But all is thick darkness to me,
    No light in the window I see;
    I've put out the light for so many—
      No light is now waiting for me!"

* * * * * * * *

(4) "Oh! had I once heeded thy voice, mother,
    When pleading in anguish with me!
    But the gold it looked bright, and the wrong it seemed right,
    And nothing but gain would I see.

Cho.—And now what is waiting for me?
No ray in the darkness I see—
I've put out the light for too many,
There's no light in the window for me!"

At the close of the song, the liquor-dealer groaned with anguish and exclaimed, "O, mother—*mother!*" Hiram felt shocked and excited; but Giovanni, calm as ever, arose from his seat and stood before the stranger. Laying his hand on the man's shoulder, he spoke in low, coaxing tones, "Give up the business—sign the Pledge—for the sake of your mother and your mother's God!"

"Oh, that I could!" exclaimed the stranger.

"You *can*, by God's grace;" replied Giovanni, "for He will help and save you, if only you will let Him do it. Then, in Heaven, you will meet your mother again!"

The liquor-dealer raised his head. The struggle was over. "I will sign it;" he said quietly; and Giovanni was delighted to see the rumseller's name go down in his Pledge-book. McRoss was greatly surprised. The gentleman made a memorandum of the name and address of his new acquaintance; and, soon, afterwards, the next stopping place was reached. The liquor-dealer clasped the hand of the young Temperance advocate, saying warmly, "God bless you, Giovanni!" and left the stage.

"It is a happy thing that you came with me;" remarked Hiram gravely; "or I should not even have known that the man was going the downward road. And now he has taken his first step homeward and heavenward!"

"Yes, thank *God* for it," said Giovanni Somerville.

CHAPTER XII.

THE TRUE CHURCH.

MISS MORRIS was surprised when the two lads entered the farm-house. "You were anxious to see that little teetotal pest—so, here he is!" said her nephew.

The old maid, notwithstanding her peculiar ways, had a kind heart. She was struck with the boy's pale face and gave him a cordial welcome. When they gathered around the fireside, that evening, there were numerous questions asked and answered. Hiram told them of his illness, of Mr. Grant's tender care, of Giovanni and Dr. Mays—and last, but not least, of the liquor-dealer signing the Pledge. Miss Morris, Sam, and old William all expressed great surprise at the latter fact. "Yes," said Hiram, "it ended well, but when that man groaned in such misery of soul, I did wish myself out of the stage!"

There was a pause. Then the young Temperance advocate spoke up suddenly, "Miss Morris, I want you to sign the Pledge."

"Me! *me!*" exclaimed the bewildered old maid, half starting out off her seat.

"Yes, *you*, madam;" said Giovanni, coolly.

Hiram and Sam laughed aloud.

"Oh, you must really excuse me."

"No, no;" said the boy, "not I indeed. You may just as well make up your mind to it, first as last, ma'am."

"My young friend," expostulated Miss Morris, "I did not pass around any liquor to-night, just out of compliment to *you*. Now, you *might* let me alone."

"I couldn't do it, ma'am. It's against my Temperance principles to let folks alone!" replied Giovanni Somerville.

Hiram laughed again at his aunt being so finely caught.

"McRoss," observed his young schoolfellow, gravely, "do be quiet." Then turning to Miss Morris, he asked, "What is your reason, ma'am, for not coming over on the Temperance side?"

The old maid would give no answer. She liked liquor, in moderation; had all her life been accustomed to use it; but did not care to give *that* as her reason. At length she hit upon the happy expedient of begging her young guest to wait until the next evening for her decision. She said it was a serious step to take and she must have time to consider.

"Very well, ma'am. But, of course, you will ask God in your prayers to-night, to show you *His* mind on the matter!"

Miss Morris was greatly surprised; but she made no reply.

"Won't you, madam?"

"Yes, *yes*; I never saw such a queer boy as you are, in all my born days!"

"Dr. Mays would agree with you there, Aunt Nell," said Hiram, laughing, "for, when a little vexed, he said *one* Giovanni was quite enough for the Seminary; aye, and by far too much!"

"I don't think any better of the doctor for that," said Miss Morris. "Now, my young friend, sing 'The Rumseller's Lament;' perchance it may do *us* good, too."

Giovanni immediately sang the piece, and they all felt solemnized by the sorrowful words. The poor old maid was troubled in conscience by it. "If liquor-sellers are such a curse to the world," she asked herself, "then are liquor-buyers and liquor-drinkers altogether blameless?" Conscience answered loudly, "No—no!"

When bed-time came, Miss Morris proposed that Giovanni should sleep with Hiram, as, at that season, the "spare-room" was too damp for an invalid; but McRoss abruptly declined to have a bed-fellow.

"My nephew, I'm ashamed of you!" said the old maid, in some perplexity what to do with her visitor.

"Do not trouble about me, ma'am," said Giovanni, "I can sleep with Sam."

"You had better not, for he is a Methodist"—playfully remarked Hiram.

"Is he? all the better;" exclaimed the young teetotaler. "The Methodists are deserving of all praise, for the noble stand they have taken in behalf of the Temperance Cause. I shall be delighted to sleep with him!"

"Indeed it is well you are so sociable," remarked the gratified Wilkins, " every one has not such an aversion to Methodists as the young boss."

"I have *no* aversion to them, Sam," was the grave

reply of McRoss. "On the contrary, Archie Campbell, my favourite school-mate, is a Methodist—and a *good* one, too!"

Giovanni smiled, as he observed, "Hiram plays and sings so many Methodist hymns, that *he* has no reason to speak against them, or, he would be apt to condemn himself. He goes to the Episcopal Church here; but, when at Roseville, to the Congregational Church, for Mr. Grant is apparently descended from the old Puritans. I wish your concertina was here, McRoss—anyway, sing your favourite hymn for us, please, a real Methodist one it is! You know that the Principal often comes into the dining-room to hear you play and sing; well, perhaps you have not noticed it, but that third verse always makes him look so grave."

"I like it very much," answered Hiram, "it need not make anyone look grave," and he sang,

> 1. My Jesus I love Thee, I know Thou art mine,
> For Thee all the pleasures of sin I resign:
> My gracious Redeemer, my Saviour art Thou—
> If ever I loved Thee, my Jesus, 'tis now.
>
> 2. I love Thee, because Thou hast first loved me,
> And purchased my pardon on Calvary's tree;
> I love Thee for wearing the thorns on Thy brow—
> If ever I loved Thee, my Jesus, 'tis now.
>
> 3. I have loved Thee in life, may I love Thee in death
> And praise Thee as long as thou lendest me breath
> And say, when the death-dew lies cold on my brow,
> If ever I loved Thee, my Jesus, 'tis now.

4. In mansions of glory, and endless delight,
I'll ever adore Thee in the heaven of light ;
And sing, with the glittering crown on my brow,
If ever I loved Thee, my Jesus, 'tis now.

" There is no wonder," remarked Giovanni, " that the third verse makes Mr. Grant feel sad—that about the cold death-dew. One time I heard him say, in a low tone, to uncle who stood by his side, "Long may it be, ere that time comes to young McRoss ! "

" I hope not ! " exclaimed Hiram, quickly.

Giovanni looked very much surprised. " Do you *wish* to die ? " he enquired. " *I* don't—not till my work is done."

" I haven't any work," said Hiram, sadly.

" Yes, you have ; *everyone* has," replied Wilkins.

" What is your's, pray ? " snapped old Billy.

" Oh," said Sam, colouring, " to commend Christianity, in general ; and the Methodist Church in particular ! "

" Then, I congratulate you on performing your work so *remarkably* well ! " sneered William.

" It's time to go to bed," said Miss Morris.

" Don't you have family prayers, ma'am ? "

" No, Giovanni ; but I have not any objection to them. Perhaps *you* will conduct them, to-night ? "

Hiram smiled, thinking it extremely unlikely; but, Giovanni, without a moment's confusion, replied, " certainly I will, if you wish it, ma'am ; only, Sam will do it so much better, that you would be wise to excuse me."

"No—no!" said Wilkins, "*you* start family worship, please; and then, *after that*, I will take it, if you choose."

"Yes, *do*;" urged the old maid. She little knew what she was asking.

"Very well, ma'am," said Giovanni, calmly, "will you let me have a Bible, please?"

One was soon handed to him, and he read aloud the twenty-third chapter of Proverbs. When he came to the verse, "look not thou upon the wine when it is red," etc., he quietly observed: "Some people may say that we have no warrant for Total Abstinence in the Scriptures—I should think that this text must be such a pricking thorn in their consciences, that they would be glad to blot it out if they could. 'When it is red—*when* it giveth its colour in the cup—*when* it moveth itself aright'—these expressions, as any chemist will tell you, clearly refer to the signs of fermentation. There are two kinds of wine spoken of in the Bible—one is fermented, and therefore contains alcohol—the other is the pure, unfermented blood of the grape—one is a curse—the other a blessing—one is the poison of dragons and the cruel venom of asps—the other is the symbol of the precious blood of Christ! The fact, that our Saviour made wine for the wedding party at Cana, has been laid hold of by our opponents. Strauss, the noted German infidel, takes it for granted that Christ made over a hundred gallons of intoxicating wine for the company, and then, of course, casts a slur on the character of our Lord. Now is it possible that the Son of God, ever anxious to do His Father's will, should provide for the guests, *fermented* wine, which that Father had declared to be 'a mocker,' and had prohibited His children from even 'looking upon it!' Friends, ask your consciences what was the nature of the wine that our Saviour made—and *never* plead His example as an excuse for indulging in the intoxicating cup." Giovanni finished reading the chapter and then calmly said, "let us pray," They all knelt down, and the young teetotaler prayed earnestly—first, for the Temperance Cause, that God would prosper it, for the glory of His own Great Name; and that it might be dear to the heart of everyone present. Then, for the family under that roof, especially for Miss Morris, that God would bless her, and give her grace to know and do her duty. The old maid was deeply touched; but, she managed to keep it to herself. When they arose, Sam abruptly announced, " I'll sign that Pledge, Giovanni."

" Oh, I'm so glad!" and the boy produced his book with pen and ink. Wilkins signed his name and then insisted on William fulfilling the promise made at Christmas. Hiram urged him, likewise, so the old man complied.

Miss Morris wished Giovanni a motherly good-night, and charged Sam to make him feel as much at home as possible.

" That I will!" returned the young man, as they went up stairs.

" What a pretty pin, Giovanni! Where did you get it?" inquired Sam, pointing to the gold ornament on Giovanni's coat.

"Mr. Grant gave it to me," said the boy, "it is a Temperance emblem, Sam. I am proud of being a soldier in the Total Abstinence ranks, and like to show my colours!"

Wilkins laughed. The warm-hearted Methodist thought that Giovanni would be an ornament to any cause, but he did not *say* so.

The following evening there was a knock at the door, Miss Morris opened it and their minister entered. After the usual salutations, he remarked "I don't wonder you all draw around the fire! What cold, damp weather we are having for the season!" Taking a seat near them, he went on, "I heard you singing the 'Star-spangled Banner,' Hiram. Is the Principal of Roseville Seminary making a Yankee of you?"

"I fear so," replied Miss Morris, smiling. "Sing a hymn for our pastor, my nephew."

Hiram sang his favourite hymn, but it was easy to see that the minister did not at all appreciate it. When it was finished, he observed, "I don't like that, my lad, it is very irreverent to speak of the Lord in such a way!"

"Do you think so, sir?" said Hiram in surprise, "I'll ask Mr. Grant if it is irreverent—indeed, I hope not, for I am very fond of it."

The parson went on, "Mr. Grant may be a very learned man, but in this case, his opinion would not be worth the paper on which it is written!"

"Why not?" demanded McRoss, indignantly.

"Because he is a Congregationalist and therefore does not belong to the *True Church*."

"The True Church!" hotly exclaimed Hiram, "I'm afraid you don't belong to it yourself, or——" Here Giovanni violently pushed his arm.

"What do you want?" asked Hiram, angrily.

"Do you think, McRoss," coolly inquired Giovanni, "that Mr. Grant would like you to go into a passion in his defence?"

"*No*," said Hiram, flushing deeply, "indeed he would not! But, Giovanni, have you not heard him say that *all* who love the Lord Jesus in sincerity (whatever denomination they may belong to) are members of His Church?"

"Yes, often," replied Giovanni Somerville. "But, one's own sense would tell one that, any way."

"You are both quite wrong—*ours* is the one True Church!" said the minister—"the one Holy, Apostolic, Catholic Church! Did not Christ pray that all His members might be *one?*"

"Mr. Grant says they *are* one, in all essential points, sir," replied McRoss.

"I am sorry he is leading you into such erroneous views, more especially as I had trained all my Sabbath scholars (to whom *you* used to belong) to believe so very differently. I don't know how to forgive Mr. Grant for the injury he is doing you."

"I cannot bear to hear you speak of him in such a way," warmly replied Hiram, "for under God, I owe to Mr. Grant my eternal salvation!"

"Oh, what shocking presumption to talk so!" exclaimed the minister, "when blessings are only promised to those who are members of the *True Church*, to which, let me tell you, the Congregationalists do not belong, nor the Methodists, either," and he glanced at Sam.

Wilkins could scarcely avoid exploding his wrath on the parson, but happily Hiram asked, in time to prevent him, " William please let me have that old book of yours, that I was reading during the last holidays. Don't trouble to go upstairs after it," he added, as the old man arose, " tell me where it is and I'll get it, myself."

" My dear young master, you are very thoughtful," said William, " the book is on that little shelf in the corner."

" Thank you," and Hiram ran up stairs and soon returned with the volume. It consisted of the bound numbers of the " Gospel Tribune." He quickly turned over the leaves until he reached the wished-for article.

"This is what that noted English Church minister, J. C. Ryle, says of the True Church, Mr. Wood. The article is long, so I will merely read a few points in it, that clearly show the writer's opinion. Listen please, all of you," and he read:

"The one true Church *is composed of all believers in the Lord Jesus.* It is made up of all God's elect,—of all converted men and women,—of all true Christians. * * * It is a Church *of which all the members have the same marks.* They are all born again of the Spirit. They all possess 'repentance towards God, faith towards our Lord Jesus Christ,' and holiness of life and conversation. They all hate sin, and they all love Christ. They worship

THE TRUE CHURCH. 149

differently, and after various fashions. Some worship with a form of prayer, and some with none. Some worship kneeling and some standing; but they all worship with one heart. They are all led by one Spirit. They all build upon one foundation. They all draw their religion from one single book, that is the Bible. They are all joined to one great centre, that is Jesus Christ. * * * This is the Church of the first-born, whose names are written in Heaven. * * * This is the 'Holy Catholic Church' of the Apostles' Creed. This is the 'One Catholic and Apostolic Church' of the Nicene Creed. This is that Church to which the Lord Jesus promises 'the gates of hell shall not prevail against it.' * * * This is the only Church which possesses true *unity*. Its members are entirely agreed on all the weightier matters of religion, for they are all taught by one Spirit. About God and Christ, and the Spirit, and sin, and their own hearts, and faith and repentance, and the necessity of holiness, and the value of the Bible, and the importance of prayer, and the resurrection and judgment to come—about all these points they are of one mind. Take three or four of them, strangers to one another from the remotest corners of the earth. Examine them separately on these points. You will find them all of one judgment. * * * This is the only Church which is truly *Catholic*. It is not the Church of any one nation or people. Its members are to be found in every part of the world where the Gospel is received and believed. It is not confined within the limits of any one country, nor pent up within the pale of any particular form of outward government. In it there is no difference between Jew and Greek, black man and white, Episcopalian and Presbyterian,—but faith in Christ is all."

Sam clapped his hands, exclaiming, "Good for Mr. Ryle; I'd like to hear him preach, first-rate—that is, just once in a while, you know. It seems there *are* some Christians in the Church of England, after all."

"Did you doubt it, Sam?" asked Hiram, with a half-laugh.

"Indeed I did!" replied Wilkins, gravely, "How could I do otherwise, young boss, when the ministers of that Church talk more of Baptism, Apostolic Succession, etc., than they do of conversion and of loving and serving Christ?"

"Some of them do, Sam;" gravely replied Hiram, "but, believe me, there are others who preach quite as evangelical sermons as does your own Methodist minister."

"That's it!" exclaimed Mr. Wood, "you've just used the right word. *Evangelicals!* They are dissenters in the Church—and J. C. Ryle is in the fore-front of them!"

Miss Morris, seeing that the parson was getting excited, adroitly changed the subject by asking a question about temperance, stating that her young visitor had urged her to sign the Pledge, and asking the advice of her pastor in the matter. The Rev. Mr. Wood warmly counselled her to bind her soul by no such vow; and then turned his wrath upon Giovanni. The boy was apparently unaffected by it; for he continued to urge Miss Morris to sign, telling her "that her own conscience would approve the act—*God* would approve it; and to all eternity she would rejoice at having taken the Pledge!"

The minister could not help admiring the lad's courage in sticking so bravely to the point. So, with a smile, he unfolded to Giovanni *his* views of the subject and this led to a general conversation which it is not necessary to repeat. The clergyman did not believe in Total Abstinence; and at length inquired "if his young friend were foolish enough to believe that the traffic in liquor would ever be put down."

"*Certainly*, sir;" replied Giovanni, "for we have One on our side who is stronger than all the rumsellers in creation!"

The old maid had always been in the habit of offering cake and wine to her minister whenever he called; she did not like to do so now, but feared he would think her lacking in courtesy if she omitted it. Therefore, she set the usual refreshments before him, and he immediately poured out a glass of wine. Giovanni sprang forward and eagerly inquired, "Will you do me a favour, sir?"

"Of course, I will;" answered the minister.

"Thank you, sir. Then, I beg that *before* you drink *that or any other* glass of intoxicating liquor, you will arise, bow your head over the poison cup, and pray, "Lord, lead us not into temptation."

The clergyman flushed crimson. He was a middle-aged man, and wine had come to have great charms for him. He knew that he liked intoxicating liquor well— knew, alas, that he had been several times the worse of it; and knew, too, that if he repeated that simple prayer, *over the wine-glass,* it would be a fearful mockery in the sight of God. He *dared* not do it; but casting an angry look at Giovanni, remarked, " I little thought what was the nature of the favour you asked, or it would never have been granted ! "

The boy earnestly answered, " Ought Christians to do anything, sir, that they *cannot* do in the Name of the Lord Jesus ? "

The minister made no reply, but left the wine untasted and soon took his leave. Miss Morris gravely looked on, her pastor had fallen below zero in her esteem, as she expressed it afterward to her Presbyterian lover, when announcing her willingness to go with him to *his* place of worship—a thing which she had always pointedly refused to do before.

The minister had just departed when Mr. Reed " dropped in." The lads rightly guessed that he was a constant visitor at the farm-house. He was inclined to Temperance already and at once signed his name in Giovanni's Pledge-book. Miss Morris could not refuse to add hers; and the following morning, all the liquor in the house was poured out in the mud and thus came to an ignominious end.

The wedding on Easter Monday was a joyful one, and the happy couple departed on their bridal tour. Hiram and Giovanni returned at once to Roseville; the former to finish the vacation with his beloved Mr. Grant, the latter with Dr. Mays. The physician welcomed his young

Temperance friend most cordially, and informed him that the Principal of Roseville Seminary had delivered a lecture on total abstinence, in the village, just after the students under his charge had gone home, and a most effective lecture it was.

The boy clapped his hands. "Oh, I'm *so* glad! He *has* 'posted' himself at last."

The poor physician could not share in the lad's joy. He said gloomily, "I hope that God has forgiven me, for the harm I have done; but Giovanni, I am getting on in life; am in my forty-third year, and therefore it is too late to sign the Pledge and become a Temperance man."

"It is *not* too late, Dr. Mays; I have read that an earnest, energetic Christian has done more for the Master, in a single year, than some sluggish Christians have done in the whole course of their lives; come over to our side, sign the pledge; go immediately to work, and, by God's blessing, you may, in the years that remain to you, do far more good than you have ever done harm."

"My dear boy, I will think it over;" and the gloomy expression on the doctor's face cleared away.

Giovanni's holidays were very happy ones. Hattie was jubilant and insisted on her father taking them out to spend a day with Aunt Alice, who was a widow lady, a sister of the doctor. She lived in the country, two miles beyond Roseville Seminary.

It was not until the last moment that the physician and Hattie took their young friend home. What mattered it to Giovanni that the two teachers and all the lads

J

were in the play-ground? He leaned over the gate as the carriage drove off, and threw a kiss to the doctor's little daughter. Hattie smiled and returned it eagerly. The boys laughed, and set up a rousing cheer, in which Mr. Slow joined, but it did not disconcert Giovanni in the least. At recess, the lads insisted on looking over his Pledge-book, and to their great surprise, they saw that the last signature was that of

George William Mays, M.D.

CHAPTER XIII.

RONALD M'FARLANE.

"SO YOU have actually succeeded in getting Dr. Mays' signature on your Pledge-book!" observed Tom Harding to Giovanni Somerville!" Allow me to congratulate you! Now try your arts of persuasion on Ronald McFarlane, the new scholar. You will find him a hard case, I fear."

"That's so," said George Thorne, "I know him well. He is very fond of his glass; and, though little older than Hiram, has been intoxicated several times. When he gets too much of the brandy bottle ——"

"*Any at all* is too much!" earnestly put in Giovanni.

"You are quite right," and Thorne smiled. "Well, when McFarlane is drunk, he is more like a wild beast than a human being—you need not laugh, Tom, I am speaking the sober truth—at best, McFarlane has a violent temper; though, happily, it is not easy to arouse it. I am really afraid of him sometimes; for when maddened by liquor, he acts like a perfect fiend."

"Then I am glad that he has come!" said Giovanni, turning to look at his new companion.

"Isn't he handsome?" asked George with a smile; "*I'm* not amiss, but freely confess that I would willingly exchange my light brown hair for his magnificent black curls. His eyes are dark and fiery as an Indian's—and are not his features most exquisitely cut?"

Tom and Giovanni laughed heartily. "Yes," replied the former, "Ronald is a fine looking fellow and no mistake. He is not only tall, but strong and muscular in proportion."

"What a splendid voice he has! He would make a good Temperance lecturer;" said Giovanni.

"I thought you intended to be one yourself."

"Certainly, Thorne; and *God helping me, so I will!*" was the earnest reply.

A week passed, and Ronald's name was not down on the Pledge-book; but, that was very far from being Giovanni's fault. The lads felt a kind of respect for the new-comer, because he was very clever, dearly loved to study—and, what was more in their eyes, made the best "captain" they had ever possessed. One day, at the dinner-table, Ronald thoughtlessly acknowledged that he had been expelled from Stirling Seminary. Mr. Grant instantly demanded the reason of his dismissal, and Ronald as promptly replied that it was for nearly killing Mr. Gibson, the young assistant teacher.

"Take care what you say!" said the Principal sternly.

"It's the truth," replied McFarlane. "Mr. Gibson kept me in one day which made me angry. As soon as I was free, I found him in the garden alone, and thrashed him so that he was insensible for over three hours. His injuries were severe, he was still in bed when I came away. The Principal urged Mr. Gibson to have me sent to the Penitentiary—but my young teacher being very forgiving, would not hear of it. It was not *his* fault that I was expelled."

"McFarlane, I don't understand how you *could* act so!" said Hiram gravely; "Was Mr. Gibson as strong as you are?"

"Oh, no—not at all. He was always very pale and thin. Indeed, there is consumption in the family, and *he* has evidently got it."

"And yet you attacked a sick man! Was that *honourable*, McFarlane?"

"No, Hiram," replied Ronald, and his cheek crimsoned, "it was *very dis*honourable. I would never have done it had I been myself!"

"I don't understand you," said the Principal.

"*I* do" emphatically remarked Giovanni, "he means that *rum* was the cause of it!"

"Yes," replied Ronald, "I was half drunk or I would never have been such a fool as to run a risk of the gallows. Why, the doctor was very much afraid that Mr. Gibson would die without recognising any of us again!"

"What a wicked, hardened wretch!" exclaimed the shocked Mr. Slow, " *do* turn him out at once!"

"That *would* be unjust," hotly exclaimed Hiram. "Give the young Scotchman a fair chance!"

Ronald McFarlane smiled at his earnestness. "I don't want to be expelled—more especially from *here* ——" he said, "for this is my last chance. Father will never think of sending me to the University, if I am unfortunate enough to get dismissed from Roseville."

"Mr. Grant is *just*. You are all right, Ronald," said Hiram McRoss.

"*Turn him out!*" shrieked Mr. Slow.

"Certainly not'—— he has been sufficiently punished,' said the Principal. He then added, "Did you part good friends with your young teacher, McFarlane?"

"Yes, sir;" and Ronald coloured. "The head-master, Mr. Gordon, took me in to see Mr. Gibson, before I went away—he was getting better, but very slowly."

"I hope they weren't stuffing wine into him!" said Giovanni, earnestly.

"Oh, no; he declined to take it. Mr. Gordon angrily commanded me to apologize to Mr. Gibson; but, I would not do it for him."

"But you parted *friends!*" observed Hiram, "will you tell us what Mr. Gibson said to you at last?"

McFarlane answered in a low voice, "He held my hand in both his own, and said, ' Good-bye, God bless you, dear Ronald.'"

There was silence on the part of teachers and scholars. It was broken by George Thorne, who gravely observed, " I always knew that MacFarlane was a great favourite with Mr. Gibson."

"Then he *might* have apologized !" snarled Mr. Slow.

"So I did, sir ; but not before Mr. Gordon. Immediately on reaching home, I wrote to Mr. Gibson and asked his forgiveness."

" I'm afraid you got it !" snarled Mr. Slow, again.

The lads laughed.

" Is Mr. Gibson a total abstainer ? " inquired Giovanni.

" Yes," replied McFarlane. " He is one of the most devoted Sons of Temperance that I ever knew. It was through him that a Division was organized in Stirling Seminary —— also, a band of Cadets. They are prospering finely ; but, Mr. Gibson cannot induce his superior to sign the Pledge."

Another week passed. Mr. Grant began to feel a very natural pride in the scholarship of Ronald McFarlane. As far as literary attainments were concerned, the young Scotchman was a pupil of whom any teacher might be proud.

" I don't like him at all !" observed the assistant to his superior, one day.

" Why not ?"

"Because," snarled Mr. Slow, "he actually knows more than I do myself!"

Mr. Grant laughed.

"I don't care!" growled his assistant, "I fairly *hate* Ronald! He is always studying natural science—of which I know nothing—(what a happy thing it is that you don't teach it, here!) and, the other night, he came stalking up to me, with some difficulty that he had failed to disentangle for himself! I knew no more about it than the man in the moon, and told him so."

Mr. Grant laughed again, and his assistant went on, "I advised the troublesome fellow to go and worry *you* with his questions—assuring him that, if he did, you would turn him out at once! I don't think he believed me!"

"I should hope not," said Mr. Grant, warmly, "is *that* a proper way to treat an earnest young student?"

Mr. Slow got up and walked out of the room. He heartily wished that McFarlane would get into trouble with Mr. Grant, but that was very far from being the intention of the young Scotchman, who conducted himself remarkably well. It was evident to both the teachers that a warm friendship was springing up between Ronald and Hiram McRoss.

The following day was one of those discouraging seasons that all teachers occasionally experience, even their best scholars failing in nearly every class. Ronald was an exception, each lesson being perfect and carefully recited. Indeed, Mr. Slow had his doubts "whether McFarlane did not know everything to begin with." The head-teacher ordered the culprits to stay in for an hour, and study; intending after tea to have an examination as to the result. At the table, the lads perceived that unpleasant news had come through the post-office. The Principal looked troubled, and was anxious to get Mr. Slow to oblige him in some way unknown to the boys; but the assistant seemed very unwilling to comply. It was evident that Mr. Grant's usually calm temper was slightly ruffled. At about seven o'clock, he came into the school-room to conduct the examination. The lads were all taken by surprise, and the majority of them were entirely unprepared. The delinquents were marched up in front of the platform, and Mr. Grant hastily wrote a problem on the black-board, and called upon Hiram to do the work. The lad came forward very unwillingly, saying in a peevish tone, "I can't do it, Mr. Grant."

"You must make the attempt; I insist upon it," and the Principal handed the chalk to McRoss, who immediately dropped it on the floor.

"Pick up that crayon this instant, and go to work," said the master sternly.

"I *won't.*"

The scholars had never known the Principal to lose his temper before. He did *now,* and gave Hiram a ringing box on the ear, angrily ordering him to go to bed. McRoss was sorry at once, for he dearly loved the Principal. Instead of leaving the room, he stooped for the chalk, and then, with tears in his eyes, humbly offered to do his best at the problem. Mr. Grant gave him a passionate box on the other ear, and told him in a stern tone to be off to bed. Hiram went a step forward, as if to obey; then suddenly turned—threw his arms around Mr. Grant, and burst out crying. The Principal was sorry now for his passionate behaviour. The anger, which ill became his calm, manly countenance, instantly passed away, and he put his arms tenderly around the big boy who was sobbing on his bosom.

"Hiram, you great baby!" snarled the assistant, with a mocking laugh, "Won't the lads torment you about this, and *so will I!* You proud fellow, do, by all means keep your face closely hidden on Mr. Grant's breast, so that *we* cannot see you cry. I never saw anything so like a whipped baby, sobbing in its mother's arms. Now, do try and hug Mr. Grant a little more tightly. My worthy superior, won't you make him look up?"

The Principal did not condescend to reply. A few minutes after he raised Hiram's head, just sufficiently to enable him to press a long, loving kiss on the forehead of " young McRoss." No words were spoken, but Hiram knew that he was fully forgiven.

"Where was the use of that?" sneered Mr. Slow; "*we* did not catch a glimpse of his face at all."

"I certainly did not intend that you should," replied the Principal coolly. " Shuter, he continued, " be good enough to do that work on the black-board."

Aleck immediately strove to comply, but, after a ten minutes' trial, confessed himself beaten. Then, the master, who was still holding Hiram clasped to him, asked

Ronald to put the work on the board, as a favour to his companions. McFarlane did so. The problem was long, and it took about fifteen minutes to accomplish the task. He then asked if the Principal wished him to explain it.

"Certainly, Ronald."

Hiram, who was comparatively calm again, raised his head. He was anxious to see the difficult problem worked out, and to hear its intricacies unravelled.

"As soon as you stop crying, young McRoss, you must go to bed."

Hiram's head drooped. He only replied, "very well, sir, I can go now. Thank you, *so much*, Mr. Grant."

The arms of the head-teacher were still around McRoss. "Don't be in a hurry, my boy," he said. Then, stroking Hiram's dark hair, he gravely continued, "I am very sorry that I struck you in a passion, young McRoss. It was very wrong. Still, I cannot remit your punishment on *that* account."

"I don't wish you to do so, sir;" and Hiram looked up in the master's face. "I will submit to anything you choose to inflict."

"Very well, my boy, you may go to bed now, but keep awake, for I ——" the Principal stopped abruptly.

"I will not get to sleep before you come, sir," and Hiram went off.

Mr. Slow at once attacked his superior as follows: "I feel perfectly delighted, Mr. Grant, to think of your getting into such a passion. To be sure, Hiram showed his bad temper, as he often does, but *you* were far the most to blame. How could you have the face to punish him when you needed it so much more yourself?"

Had Mr. Slow not been well acquainted with the calm, Christian forbearance which shone so brightly in the Principal he would not have dared to use such language. Mr. Grant did not choose to defend himself—his assistant could not reproach him more than his own conscience had done. To *some* teachers a fit of unseemly anger is of almost daily occurrence, but neither assistant, scholar nor servant had seen Mr. Grant lose his temper before. The Principal was naturally dignified and reserved; but it was not the thought of being lowered in the eyes of his scholars that troubled him. No—it was the disgrace that his fit of passion had brought on the cause of Him whom he loved and served.

As there was no answer, Mr. Slow boldly continued, "A fine Christian, aren't you! Often have you scolded Hiram for not controlling his temper—'tis a pity, indeed, that there is no one to scold *you!* I lately read that Christians have the best Master in the universe. Don't you think that you have 'disappointed His expectation' to-night? And yet I don't doubt that you love Him."

Mr. Grant's face showed that he felt the home-thrust deeply. The keen eyes of the young Scotchman noticed the quiver, only just perceptible, of the master's lip, and he immediately interposed, by saying loudly and impatiently, "How much longer are we to stand here, Mr. Slow? Perhaps you would like to explain this problem yourself—if so, here's the chalk."

"I'll not do it!" and the assistant walked off,

McFarlane took his time over the explanations, for reasons best known to himself, and, as soon as they were finished, Mr. Slow returned to the attack.

"*You* are not the judge, my assistant," answered the Principal, calmly.

"Do you mean that you acted right?" growled Mr. Slow.

"Did you not hear me tell young McRoss that it was very wrong?" asked the master. "I only meant that *you* are not the Judge—not the One to whom we must give account."

"I would *like* to hear you give it."

The light that shone on Mr. Grant's face was beautiful as he replied reverently. "*Thou* shalt answer for me, O Lord, my God!"

"*Mr. Slow can't say that!*" triumphantly exclaimed Ronald McFarlane.

"*No*," growled the assistant, and he hurried out of the room.

"Now, we must finish this examination, boys," said the master; and he accordingly summoned Giovanni and Archie, who were free, to work two short problems on the board, while he busied himself with a third, more difficult than either. When they were completed, without any explanation, he inquired of Shuter whether he understood the work.

"Not Giovanni's," said Aleck, "for I can't conceive what he means by those letters $C_2 H_6 O$."

Giovanni darted forward at once to rub them out, but

was prevented by Mr. Grant. Ronald laughed, while the other lads looked puzzled, for chemistry was not taught in the Seminary.

"McFarlane, what is the meaning of $C_2 H_6 O$?" asked the master.

"It is the symbol for ethylic or common alcohol, sir," answered Ronald, half laughing.

"Giovanni, do you know much of chemistry?"

"No, sir—I wish I did."

"*I* can help you *a little*," answered Ronald, eagerly. "If you want assistance from that delightful science in your temperance studies my chemical cabinet is at your service."

Giovanni's large brown eyes opened widely with pleasure as he expressed his thanks. "And you have retorts, test tubes, etc.?" he eagerly inquired.

"Certainly;" and Ronald smiled.

"What is the meaning of those letters, Giovanni?" asked the master.

"Oh, sir, it just means that the compound which we call ethylic alcohol is made up of two parts of carbon, six parts of hydrogen and one part of oxygen, chemically combined together."

"Quite right; but why did you put it on the blackboard?"

"O, Mr. Grant my head ached—and beside that, I am sorry to say, that I was thinking of something else."

"Very well, I excuse you. The problem is correctly worked, with that exception."

Giovanni returned to his seat, feeling thankful that he had escaped reproof for his carelessness.

When the lads were sent off to bed, Ronald went into Hiram's room. McRoss was lying in his usual position, viz: with the pillow pulled down beside him, his arms around it and his cheek resting against it. McFarlane smiled. "Do you always hug your pillow after that fashion?" he inquired.

"Oh, yes, it's only a habit."

"McRoss," asked Ronald abruptly, "why does not the head-teacher get a new assistant?"

"From pity to Mr. Slow, who is so peevish and hateful, that if even he succeeded in obtaining another situation (which is doubtful) he would not keep it for a week?"

"It is very good and Christian-like of Mr. Grant."

"*Very*," responded Hiram, warmly, "and the assistant has often owned it, but that does not prevent him from being extremely snappish to his superior. Ronald, it is against the rules for you to come in here."

"Why didn't you tell me that before? Good-night."

A few minutes later Mr. Grant came up stairs. The young Scotchman was standing at the door of his room. "I went in to see McRoss, sir, having no idea that it was against the rules. Will you kindly excuse me this time?"

"Oh, yes, McFarlane, it's all right," and the Principal passed on, entered his favourite's apartment and locked the door. Then he sat down on the side of the bed, and Hiram pushing away his pillow laid his head on Mr. Grant's lap. That gentleman stroked the lad's curly hair, and with flushed cheeks and an evident effort said, " young McRoss, I want your forgiveness."

" I've nothing to forgive! you did not hurt me the one-twentieth part of what I deserved."

" Perhaps not; but I struck you in passion, not for punishment, not to do you good. Say that you forgive me, young McRoss."

" I don't want to;" answered Hiram, reproachfully. " *You*, the head-master to ask pardon of a scholar; you say you are proud," he added sadly, " did it hurt you to ask that?"

The master replied in a low voice, " yes."

" Then *why* do you do it, sir?" inquired Hiram in a tone of distress.

" Because it was *right*, young McRoss, it will hurt me worse if you don't say it. Won't you, just to satisfy me?"

Hiram burst into tears, it hurt *him* the worst after all. He could only sob, " I forgive you, Mr. Grant."

" My poor child," said the master, " I did not mean to distress you;" and he wiped the tears off his favourite's face. " Why are you lying with your head down here?" he continued.

" Because sir, I felt that I was in disgrace."

" Then I can sympathize with you, my boy," said Mr. Grant, sadly, " for *I* too feel that I am deeply in disgrace."

" How do you mean, sir;" asked Hiram in a low voice —" with God?"

" *Yes;*" replied the Principal, and he told his favourite

of what Mr. Slow had said—" Christians have the best Master in the universe. Don't you think that you have disappointed His expectation to-night? And yet, I don't doubt that you love Him!" The voice of the Principal was husky and his eyes were full of tears as he added, " Indeed I *do* love him. It matters little what the scholars think of me; but, oh, I am so sorry that I have grieved my Saviour."

" Dear Mr. Grant, *tell Him so*!" and Hiram raised himself from his lowly position and leaned on the master's breast.

The Principal smiled sadly. " Well, it is some comfort that I can do *that*, young McRoss."

" Pray for me, too, please;" said Hiram, as Mr. Grant knelt down by the bedside, " for I need it far more than you do."

The Principal did so.

At that moment, Ronald was in his room, with the door securely locked. He was sitting at the table, with a glass of brandy-and-water in his hand. He always chose the evening, now, for indulging his appetite for liquor. Several times he had had his stock surreptitiously replenished, through the means of the old house-keeper, who was not above being bribed. Ronald was the only child of wealthy parents, who kept him liberally supplied with money. They thought that he expended it mainly for books, philosophical apparatus, etc., and they were not mistaken. Still, there remained a considerable margin for rum and brandy. Ronald was generally careful not to exceed, for

fear of expulsion; but this evening, for the third time
since his arrival at Roseville, he drank to partial intoxication. On each occasion, he went to bed as soon as possible, to avoid suspicion; and the next morning awoke,
with nerves unstrung, and a dreadful headache. How he
longed for just *one* glass of brandy, to steady himself;
but that he dared not take for fear of discovery. Some
boy would be sure to detect the alcoholic fumes in his
breath—or, the teachers, even, find out his disgrace.

"You're not eating any breakfast, McFarlane," said
the assistant, snappishly, " Have you got headache again?"

"Yes, sir," was the weary answer.

"Well, I'm not the least sorry for you. It's all your
own fault."

Ronald coloured.

" You're just as bad as Mr. Grant," went on the assistant, " *he* used to be troubled with fearful headaches continually, and no wonder. Oh, how many times have I
arisen from my bed, at midnight or past, because I was
sure that ghosts were around; but the ghost always turned
out to be Mr. Grant who was stalking upstairs to bed at
that unseasonable hour, having been unable to tear himself away from his beloved books before. Science is all
very well; but he need not study himself to death ! And
when he *did* get as far as his room door, it was invariably
with a lamp in one hand and a couple of books in the
other. How much longer he read, I'm sure I don't know.
Of course, Ronald, I was never in the least sorry for him,

when he suffered the consequences; and neither am I for *you!*"

McFarlane coloured. "Oh, that *my* headaches had as innocent a cause as those of the master!" he thought to himself.

"You study far too hard," went on Mr. Slow.

"I don't think so, sir."

"It would be wise to take care of yourself, Ronald," said one of the boys.

"I know it, Archie; and so I do, in most things."

"Yes, of course," growled Mr. Slow; "well, go on and study, all day and all night, too, for anything it matters to me; but you will be apt to die of brain fever—or, awake some fine morning to find yourself in the lunatic asylum!"

"That will do, my assistant. Ronald is evidently ill; and I won't allow him to be teased!"

Mr. Slow snarled out, "Very likely he is ill. No matter; I don't care. The idea of your asking me to take the entire charge of those lads, for four whole days, until you go to Kingston and settle that worrying affair. I'll not do it."

"'Tis a pity that you think it such a trouble," said Mr. Grant, dryly.

"I would not take charge of Ronald for a single day, no matter what inducement you offered me."

"Oh, Mr. Grant, are you going away?" asked Hiram, sorrowfully.

"I *ought* to, young McRoss. My lawyer cannot manage the affair without me. It will be quite a sacrifice if ——"

"Do you mean to say, you rich, old Yankee, that the loss will be felt by you in the least?"

"Personally—no; but my assistant, you forget that I am only a steward, and have to give account of all moneys committed to my trust."

"Why, I thought the whole estate belonged to you."

"Mr. Slow," said Hiram, "how can you be so obtuse? Mr. Grant is a steward of our God in Heaven."

The assistant snarled out, "That's all very fine. Well, I'm sorry if you lose, but it cannot be helped. I'll not have anything to do with that odious McFar——."

"Mr. Grant," broke in Hiram, "leave *Ronald* in charge. He will do splendidly; for he is far more fit to teach than to learn."

"*Do!*" echoed Mr. Slow, sarcastically, "and I'll take holiday and be off for a few days. Giovanni will have to stay here."

"I'll be all right, uncle."

"What say *you*, McFarlane?" and Mr. Grant smiled.

"I'm not fit to teach, sir—do not know enough yet."

"You are mistaken," answered the Principal; "your knowledge is amply sufficient. Will you take full charge during the four days of our absence?"

"I will do the best that I can if you choose to trust me, sir," replied Ronald.

"Very good; then I will take the stage this morning.

Give the boys a holiday if you do not feel able to teach, to-day."

"I'll manage, sir."

"All right; I am exceedingly obliged to you."

While the head-master and his assistant packed their respective valises, Ronald went up to his room, took pen and paper, and wrote in a nervous, shaky hand:

"I solemnly promise not to drink one drop of intoxicating liquor during the four days' absence of the Principal.

"RONALD MURRAY MCFARLANE."

He then bathed his head with cold water and went down stairs. Soon afterwards the two teachers drove off, and he was left in full charge of Roseville Seminary.

CHAPTER XIV.

THE PUPIL TEACHER.

THE morning lessons proceeded as usual, and the greater part of the lads conducted themselves well. The younger boys were instructed by monitors, under Ronald's supervision. What he suffered that morning was best known to himself. His head ached dreadfully, and the responsibility seemed more than he could bear. As the day wore on he felt somewhat better. One or two of the lads were inclined to be impertinent, and more especially Tom Harding, who declined to submit to the authority of the young teacher. Ronald kept his temper bravely, but he knew that he must quell the first attempt at insubordination, and therefore flogged Mr. Tom rather severely with a big, willow switch. The scholars saw that he was not to be trifled with, and there was no further attempt to dispute his authority.

In the evening, he remained in the school-room, to correct the scholars' exercise-books. While thus employed, he came to Giovanni's, and was surprised to find a number of neatly-written notes on the subject of total abstinence. He turned over the leaves to discover the exercise portion of the book, but, instead of that, alighted on a piece of original poetry. Poor Ronald! he was longing for a glass of brandy, and did not at all appreciate the verse or two that he read. " Miserable doggerel," he muttered to himself, and immediately turned on. But three or four lines fixed themselves indelibly in his memory:

" May Thy favour, most precious Lord Jesus,
    Thy blessing, to me be given ;
    Let me carry Thy Temperance Banner
    To the very gate of Heaven."

The words rang through McFarlane's brain. " I've no doubt he will do it," muttered the young Scotchman to himself. " He will carry the temperance banner as long as he lives on earth—or, as *he* expresses it, ' to the very gate of Heaven.' Giovanni!" he called, and the lad immediately approached.

"Aren't you afraid that the teachers will read your notes, poetry, &c. ?"

"Oh, no; they would not think it worth while. Besides, if they *did*, there's nothing to hurt them."

Ronald smiled in spite of himself. "No, I don't believe there is. That will do; you may go. I see where the exercise is now."

"Oh, dear," muttered the young teacher, as Giovanni went back to his companions, "I do wish that I had never read those wretchedly-composed lines."

All proceeded as usual until the clock struck nine. At that hour Mr. Grant invariably assembled the lads in the dining-room for prayers, before sending them to bed.

"*I* can't pray," thought McFarlane, "and yet, how can I conscientiously dismiss them for the night without family worship—what in the world am I to do?"

Just then Hiram came up to the platform, and Ronald asked, in a low voice, "McRoss, if I read a chapter, will you pray?"

Hiram coloured deeply. "I couldn't. It is as much as I can do to pray for myself."

There was a pause, and then a sudden thought striking McRoss, he said, "*Giovanni* will do it, if you ask him; but it will be a *Temperance* prayer, of course."

"I don't want one," returned Ronald, almost fiercely. "Ivon, come this way," he called, adding to his companion, "Perhaps our little ten-year-old minister can help us out of our difficulty."

The child immediately came forward, and McFarlane asked the same question of him as he had of Hiram.

"Oh, teacher! do read us some of the Collects in our Book of Common Prayer. Where can you find anything more beautiful?"

At this moment, Giovanni came up, and McFarlane answered gravely, "I never pray, Ivon. If I read those collects I should not mean them—and, therefore, it would be hypocrisy and mocking God."

"O! Ronald," said the child, "don't you want to be saved?"

"*Yes*," replied McFarlane, earnestly; "but the wicket gate, though wide enough to admit *me*, is too narrow to admit my *sin*, and I cannot give it up."

"Yes, you can, by God's grace," replied Giovanni Somerville.

"But I don't ask it," said McFarlane, gravely. "If it were not for *one thing* I should have been a Christian long ago, as all you three are. *I cannot be saved because the rum-bottle stands between my soul and Heaven!*"

"Oh, Ronald! Ronald! give up the accursed thing."

"Indeed, *indeed*, Giovanni, I wish I could. Ivon, get your book and read those prayers for us. I cannot, *dare* not do it!"

The child hesitated not to comply, though he could not help saying to himself, "McFarlane would do it far better."

The struggle that Ronald had with his evil nature before going to bed may be imagined, but he resisted the strong temptation of the brandy-bottle, though the want of his accustomed stimulant kept him awake for hours. The following morning he felt somewhat better, and the house-keeper, unknown to the other lads, made some strong coffee for him, so that he was able to teach with more comfort than on the previous day.

Immediately after recess, in the forenoon, Ronald ordered the boys to put every book in their desks—take a sheet of foolscap paper, and write a composition then and there. The scholars looked uneasy, for they invariably wrote their themes, etc., in the evenings, and many of them got far too much help from one another and from books. There was no hope of assistance from either of these sources with Ronald's keen eyes upon them. They waited somewhat anxiously for the subject. When all were ready, McFarlane announced "The compositions are to be on Alcohol!"

It was amusing to witness the consternation with which one scholar gazed on another, but Ronald did not smile—he was as grave as a judge. There was only *one* bright face among the group of boys, and that was Giovanni's. He was well acquainted with the subject, and felt confident that he could write his composition well. The other lads, not caring to offend Ronald, did their best, which was very poor after all. Nearly all the themes were definitions of the word alcohol—some very short and some longer. Archie and Ivon wrote a few words on the moral view of the subject, while Giovanni, in the allotted time, filled three pages of foolscap. Shuter stared at his industrious companion, especially when the latter drew a plain diagram to illustrate "distillation," which process wȧs fully described in the composition. Ronald expressed his pleasure on examining Giovanni's work. He read the themes aloud; for the most part it was easily done. Some merely defined alcohol as a drug, others as a poison, others as the spirit contained in ale, wine, beer, etc., while Archie's and Ivon's spoke of the evil caused by the stuff. Giovanni commenced his composition with a full description of alcohol, mentioned the various proportions contained in different liquors, described and illustrated the process of distillation, stated some scientific facts concerning the "accursed thing," that it is neither food nor fuel—never gives strength nor health; in fact is, as Giovanni asserted, "only evil continually." In conclusion, he spoke of the misery and ruin in which it involves both the bodies and souls of its wretched victims. To the dismay of the lads, Ronald declared his intention of showing the compositions to Mr. Grant, and accordingly locked them up in that gentleman's desk.

Shortly before the time of dismissal at four o'clock, a grammar class recited. It was evident that several of the scholars had not studied the lesson at all. Among them were Hiram and Shuter. McFarlane did not scold —he only said, " McRoss, report yourself to Mr. Grant— the others will remain in after school until they repeat that lesson perfectly."

When the exercises for the day closed, Hiram walked

up to the platform and said, gravely, "I wish you would keep me in, Ronald."

"You must report yourself to the head-master."

"It is too bad! You might treat me the same as the others. The Principal will think that I was mean enough to take advantage of his absence."

"Oh, no; the Principal knows right well the careless manner in which you usually study."

"*Won't* you keep me in?"

"No," replied Ronald, firmly; "you are Mr. Grant's pet, and I don't intend to punish you if it is possible to help it."

Hiram went off, sadly enough, resolving to have no more missed lessons to "report" to the head-teacher. "I'll learn *this* well, at all events," he said to himself, and carried his book upstairs, where he faithfully studied it.

As McFarlane was sitting at the master's desk that evening, Giovanni took his Pledge-book and earnestly entreated the pupil-teacher to sign his name.

"Why are you so anxious about me?" was the impatient reply.

"Oh, Ronald," said the boy, sorrowfully, "I have thought of you all day. Last night it was impossible to sleep after what you told us. For the love of your father and mother—for the love of that young teacher, Mr. Gibson—above all, for the love of Christ give up the rum-bottle!"

McFarlane bowed his head on his hands. "Giovanni, *I can't do it,*" he groaned. "Would to Heaven that I could."

"Ronald, Ronald, do you suppose that the Most High God cannot give you power to take that solemn oath and keep it, too? It is astonishing to me that you, who are so deeply interested in the natural sciences, especially astronomy, should doubt the omnipotence of Jehovah! Not for a moment will I believe that the glorious Creator, who made all those bright suns and worlds that you were pointing out to us the other night, cannot enable you to keep your pledge. 'The Lord's hand is not shortened that it cannot save.' You say there is nothing else that prevents you from being a Christian."

"Indeed," was the low answer, "had it not been for *that*, I would have yielded myself to the Redeemer long ago. Mr. Gibson was so anxious that I should be saved —I know he prays for me, though it is more than I do for myself."

"Do you mean to say," said Giovanni, gently, "that you intend to throw back the love of the Lord Jesus in his face?"

"I can't help it," replied Ronald, huskily. "I can't *help* it."

Further conversation was prevented by Shuter coming up and asking McFarlane to explain a difficulty in his Latin translation. Very patiently was Master Aleck assisted, and when he went back to his comrades he expressed a decided opinion that Ronald was a "right good fellow."

"I *know* it," emphatically returned George Thorne. "*Much* do I admire McFarlane, and like him well, too. There is only one thing against him, and that is *drink*."

"Work hard, Giovanni, and make him sign, if you can," urged Shuter. "He is a noble fellow, and well worthy of your efforts."

"I know it, Aleck. Indeed I will do my best."

"It would not be you if you did not," said George Thorne, merrily. He then added more gravely, "There is, however, a boy here that I admire and like more than Ronald, and that is Hiram McRoss."

Laughs and looks of surprise followed. "Indeed, you amaze me," said Reynolds, "of course we *like* Hiram, he is popular among us, but—but there is nothing to *admire* about him."

"Why not?" was angrily demanded.

"Oh, he is so hot-tempered, and is constantly getting into some trouble or other——"

"You make it worse than it is," remarked Aleck; "Hiram has improved greatly since he became a Christian—remember it is only about a year and a half ago. Surely you don't expect McRoss to have become a full-grown saint in that short time?"

"Reynolds professes to be a Christian himself; but I am sure that Hiram is a far better one," said Thorne, warmly.

"Well, it's too bad," put in Tom, "there are far more saints, or *would-be* saints, among us than I like. What a disagreeable thing that we should have so many religious persons in the Seminary. I never thought that Hiram would become one of the 'praying set,' but he *has*—thanks to that precious Mr. Grant of his—and now

I really believe that it would be easier to make water run up-hill, than it would to make McRoss do anything that he thinks wrong—except, of course, you can manage to get him mad—then he will do most anything."

"Yes," said Archie, warmly, "and bitterly he repents of it afterwards. But you go too far, Tom—even when angry, McRoss will *not* do 'most anything.' No matter if you do provoke him to get into a passion, he never strikes one of you even then, nor says a bad word. Often and often did he do both before his conversion. He is naturally of a fiery temper, Tom, and well you know it —pray remember, when you draw him into sin, what a fearful account you are laying up against yourself."

"Just stop, you Methodist preacher; I don't care a snap what you say!"

"You will care sometime, Tom," said Ivon, in a tone of distress, as he clasped his arms around Harding's waist.

The latter replied calmly, "If they were all like *you*, child, and Giovanni, I should think more of Christians than I do. Thorne," he added, in a mocking tone, "didn't you admire Hiram the other night, when he burst out crying because Mr. Grant boxed his ears?"

"It's a burning shame you won't hold your tongue!" exclaimed George, hotly. "How often have you teased McRoss about it already. I was so glad that he did not get angry."

"He looked very much ashamed, though," said Tom. "Hiram, you're just in time."

"For what?" inquired McRoss, who had at that moment come up.

"Oh," replied Harding, "Thorne had been expressing his admiration of you, so I just reminded him of the other night, when you burst out crying because Mr. Grant slapped you. Don't you think," added the boy, laughing, "that Thorne had good reason to admire you then?"

Hiram's cheeks burned. He was quite able to thrash Master Tom, but conscience would not suffer him to do it. He replied at length, gravely enough :

"I guess that George was only in fun. There is nothing whatever to admire in me at any time."

"Did not you feel bad to break down in such a way?" inquired Reynolds.

There was no answer, so he continued impatiently:

"Didn't you feel bad when Mr. Grant put his arms around you?"

"Oh," replied Hiram, with a smile, "*that* made me feel better."

The boys laughed, and Tom remarked scornfully,— "Weren't you glad when he kissed you?"

"*Very* glad," answered Hiram.

"Do you know, McRoss," went on Tom, "that Archie has quite forgotten how you cut open his cheek? He said just now that you never strike any of us, though we *do* make you angry."

"That was an exception," said James Bell. "You ought to be ashamed to mention it, Tom."

"Oh, I only wanted to get Hiram into a passion."

"I don't see what good *that* would do you," calmly replied McRoss.

"My dear fellow," said Thorne, "I would not be made angry by him."

"O, George!" was the earnest answer, "if you had my hateful temper you would see how hard it is to help it."

"It *must* be," said the sympathizing Thorne; "but, Hiram, you are doing bravely. I am sure that you pleased your Master to-night."

"Thank you," was the low answer, "I *tried* to," and he went away.

"McRoss is a queer fellow," said Tom. "I wonder if Mr. Grant whipped him that night?"

"Oh, no," replied George.

"Then why did he tell him to keep awake?"

"I guess he wanted to talk to him; anyway, Mr. Grant neither flogged nor scolded him, for I asked McRoss myself. What the master *did* say I don't know; for Hiram would not tell me."

"There's the bell for prayers;" said Tom, "I think Ronald might have safely omitted them! Now you need not look so horrified Archie; you might say a double amount upstairs, if you chose instead!"

"O Tom, you should not talk so!" said Giovanni, sorrowfully.

Harding did not reply; he could not speak crossly to his young Temperance comrade, of whom he was very fond.

That night when all was still, Ronald McFarlane's resolution apparently failed him, for he produced a tumbler and a bottle of brandy. "It's no use talking; I can't resist;" he said to himself, " of course it is dishonourable to break one's word, aye, and dreadfully wicked, too, for the promise was made to *God!* And then, the Principal reposed such confidence in me, that he left everything in my hands, and I said that I would do my best. Would this be my best? *No!* What would Mr. Gibson say if I broke my word?" At this point, McFarlane drew out a letter which he had received a few days previous from his former young teacher. It was written in a trembling hand, and with good reason, for the writer was propped up in bed with pillows to be able to do it. The tender words of love touched the heart of McFarlane and the prayer, with which the letter concluded, settled the matter for that night at least. Ronald folded up the note and placed it in his breast pocket. He then arose and hastily thrust the brandy bottle and tumbler out of sight. "God help me!" he softly uttered, and began to prepare for bed.

On the following morning, Giovanni asked McFarlane to teach them a little chemistry, "You know, Ronald," he added, "that yesterday you gave us a lesson in botany; and, the day before, one in zoology, which interested the boys greatly. Do give us some chemistry to-day!"

"Very well. What part is it you wish?"

"I want to see how you distil things." Please put a spoonful of salt into water and let it dissolve, and then drive off the water by heating it in a glass retort."

"All right. I will arrange the apparatus and you shall perform the experiment for yourself."

Ronald was as good as his word. He gave the whole school a short lesson in chemistry and then saw that Giovanni distilled a glass of salt water, without breaking the retort or doing other damage.

In the afternoon a new scholar made his appearance. Ronald admitted him conditionally, until the return of the Principal. He was older than Hiram—probably about twenty-two—but thin and delicate looking. On being questioned by the lads, he stated that his name was William Manning, and that he had been sickly for a long time. However, he was much better now and wished to have the advantage of another year at school. Giovanni at once pressed him to sign the Pledge and thus join the "noble Temperance army," but Mr. Manning declined "just at present," for reasons which he did not seem willing to tell.

"I am so glad that Mr. Grant is coming home, to-morrow;" said Hiram, at the supper-table, that evening.

"So am I!" thought Ronald, but he did not say it—alas, he wished for the return of the Principal, because *then* he would be free from his promise of abstinence.

"Of course you're glad, McRoss;" remarked Tom, "I wonder how you manage to sleep at all now, without the master poking into your room every night. Some of the boys wonder why he never misses—but, he doubtless goes in to hear you say your prayers!"

Several of the lads laughed. Hiram did not reply, though his face reddened. Ever since that dreadful night when he had been carried by Giant Despair into doubting castle, Mr. Grant helped him as he had never done before. Instead of just coming into his favourite's room and kissing him a fatherly good-night as had been his previous custom, the Principal would invariably sit by the bedside for half an hour or so, relieving the lad's mind from any difficulty and giving words of comfort, counsel and encouragement. If reproof were necessary, it was always very gently administered. Those precious evening moments, with Mr. Grant, were sacred things to Hiram; and he felt that the boys had no right to question him about them.

"I would like to hear the prayers of McRoss;" said Giovanni gravely, "for about half of them would doubtless be for blessings on the head of the Principal!"

"And three-fourths of *yours*," retorted Hiram, "would be for the success of the Temperance cause!"

The boys laughed. "Good for you, McRoss!" said George Thorne. "Now you can't deny it, Giovanni!"

"Deny it!" and the big brown eyes of the young Temperance advocate opened widely, "why ever should I wish to deny it?"

The boys laughed again. Tom impatiently observed, "He may pray for the good cause if he likes—that won't hurt!"

"Why won't you sign the Pledge, Willie Manning?" asked Giovanni.

"Well, you *do* corner me," said the new comer, who was very simple-minded. (The boys thought him "soft," but changed their views before the week was out.)

"You *do* corner me," he went on. "But the truth is, I'm engaged to be married, and my—my—well, my young lady might not like it."

The boys burst into a merry laugh which evidently surprised Mr. Manning exceedingly. He went on, quite enthusiastically, "If you could only see the little darling for yourselves, I'm sure you would all envy my happiness!"

The lads went off into another roar, and even Ronald could with difficulty keep his countenance straight. He asked, "What has *that* to do with your signing the pledge?"

"Why, do you suppose I would think of such a thing without first consulting *her!*"

"Are you really in earnest, Will?" asked Giovanni; who thought that his comrade was perhaps playing them a trick.

"In earnest! Of course I am! I'll show you Rosa's photograph after tea."

"*Do*," responded Tom Harding, with mock gravity. "I only hope we shall not all feel dreadfully jealous of your good fortune."

When the lads were once more in the school-room, they called on Manning to fulfil his promise.

"Certainly," said that young gentleman; "but I must give you a description of her first. She is a little chunk of a thing, with a round face, rosy cheeks and a lot of darkish hair, which she wears combed straight back from her forehead, and tied in a big bunch behind—something as the Chinamen wear theirs."

The boys could not restrain their mirth, which vexed Will, and he said, "If you can't stop that nonsense I'll not say another word about the little dear ——."

A second burst of merriment cut him short. "I never did see such asses in all my life!" exclaimed the disgusted Mr. Manning. "But as I promised to show you the photograph, I will do so." So saying, he produced the likeness of a young lady, observing warmly, "This is Rosa Wright." None of them could say anything unpleasant of that pretty, merry, little face, and the owner of the treasure looked well pleased at the admiration expressed in the lads' words. Giovanni congratulated the doating lover and then remarked, "But I don't see *why* you can't sign the pledge without asking her opinion in the matter."

"It won't be long before she answers my letter. I've got it written. If she thinks well of it you may count upon my name."

"Of course she will advise you to sign," observed Tom Harding.

"I'm very much mistaken if she is not dead against Temperance pledges," said Mr. Manning.

"Then, I would like to box Rosa Wright's ears," muttered Giovanni Somerville.

CHAPTER XV.

MR. GRANT'S RETURN TO ROSEVILLE.

MR. GRANT duly arrived at noon the next day, which was Saturday. He was much pleased that things had gone on so well in his absence, for he would be obliged to go away again during the following week. Mr. Slow had prophesied all kinds of evil. On examining the lads, the Principal was fully satisfied in his own mind, that McFarlane had instructed them remarkably well. Hiram with reddening cheeks, told Mr. Grant of his "missed lesson," but that gentleman was lenient, and finding that he knew it thoroughly, did not even keep him in.

That evening Ronald was called into the library-parlor, where the Principal was sitting alone. " McFarlane," he remarked; " you have done me a great favour, and, as I cannot offer you money without insulting you—for it is evident that you don't need it—will you tell me whether I can be of service to you in any other way ? "

" Did I satisfy you, sir ? "

" Yes, you did indeed."

" I'm very glad, Mr. Grant. As I am writing home to-night, would you kindly send a few lines to my father saying that I have behaved tolerably well since coming here."

The Principal laughed. " I can conscientiously give

you a better recommendation than *that*, McFarlane;" he said; and going to his desk, he wrote a note to Ronald's father, speaking highly of his son. Mr. Grant particularly mentioned the fact of McFarlane's supplying *his* place and doing it so well.

"I am *very* much obliged to you, sir; but you ought not to have spoken so favourably of me;" said Ronald, gratefully, as he took the paper and went out.

The following morning was clear and bright. Ronald's headaches were apparently becoming chronic. He looked really ill, on coming down to breakfast.

"McFarlane, you have over-exerted yourself. I'm afraid;" said the head-master, noticing that Ronald's hand trembled violently as he raised the cup of coffee to his lips.

"My head aches, Mr. Grant; it was not with teaching, however."

"I fear you are mistaken, McFarlane," replied the Principal, "it must have been a great strain upon you, for you took all the most difficult classes."

"Can't you eat anything at all?" inquired Mr. Slow. "Why your headaches get worse all the time. The lunatic asylum is in store for you yet!"

"My assistant, I will not allow it," said the Principal, sternly, "understand *that!*"

After breakfast, Ronald was lying on his bed, when he was startled by a gentle footstep and a hand tenderly laid on his shoulder.

"McFarlane, you are killing yourself!" said George

Thorne. He was the only scholar who knew the cause of Ronald's headaches. As for the teachers, they had not the remotest suspicion of anything wrong.

"I can't help it!" bitterly exclaimed McFarlane. "Are you going to tell the Principal?"

"I don't want to; but oh, Ronald, *why* won't you stop drinking?"

"That's easily answered, Thorne. Because I can't!"

"McFarlane, why don't you ask God to help you?"

"What do *you* know about His help?" inquired Ronald, much surprised.

"Nothing personally, but I'm afraid we both need it above everything else."

"Thorne, do leave me alone. I'm just distracted *now*, and mind you don't tell Mr. Grant."

" But—suppose he asks me?"

"Why, speak the truth, of course! Only don't tell unless he *does* inquire."

"I'm not likely to do *that*. O, Ronald, I wish you were saved!" and George hastily left the room, saying bitterly to himself, "That fine fellow is just going to ruin—everlasting ruin—and, what is more, with his eyes wide open."

Mr. Manning was taking notes in his own mind as to the characters of the different lads. On Monday morning, before school, he gravely asked of Hiram, "whether all Christians loved Jesus best."

" Of course they do!"

" Is Giovanni a Christian?"

" Why, *yes*—how can you doubt it?" asked Hiram in surprise.

"I don't believe that he loves any one so well as that phantom thing!"

"What do you mean?"

"Why that *phantom of a thing* that he calls '*the Cause.*'"

Hiram laughed. " Indeed Will, Giovanni would be the opposite of pleased if you told him that the Temperance Cause is a phantom thing!"

"Well, doesn't he love it better than all else beside?"

"Not better than Christ;" gravely returned McRoss.

" You're mistaken, Hiram. The lad is there at his desk, reading, instead of out-doors where he *ought* to be. Come here Giovanni," he called, and the lad approached, book in hand.

"Is there anything you love better than the Temperance Cause?" inquired Manning.

"*No!*" replied Giovanni, with a look of surprise at such a question.

" Now, McRoss, am I not right?"

" Oh, no;" answered Hiram. Then, addressing Giovanni, he demanded, " Is there no one—*person*—that you love more than the Temperance Cause,"

" Oh, if you put it in *that* way;" said Giovanni, "of course I love our Captain better than our cause! But, it is only fair to say that they are so connected in my mind that I rarely think of one without the other."

" I was just telling Hiram that it is a phantom thing."

" The Temperance Cause a phantom thing!" indignantly exclaimed Giovanni ——" Why, there could not be a greater reality! It is *God's* cause. Never you dare to say that again, Will Manning!" and the lad walked off.

"I was wrong;" said the new comer, "he *does* love Christ the best; though I'm sure I did not think so."

"I was certain of it; for, I have known him for over two years."

"Mr. Grant," said Hiram, as he was lying in bed on the evening before that gentleman went away for the second time, "the minister, at Oakville, said that my favourite hymn was irreverent —— do *you* think so?"

The Principal stroked Hiram's hair caressingly, as he answered, "Oh, no, young McRoss."

"I did not believe it, sir; but, *he* said it was——to speak of the Lord in such a way! The words 'My Jesus,' I suppose were the ones he disapproved of."

"Probably they were, my boy. Would it be irreverent to say, 'My Saviour?'"

"Oh, no, sir. That expression is a Bible one! Mary says 'My Spirit hath rejoiced in God, my Saviour.'"

"Very good. Now, young McRoss, our English word 'Saviour,' is Joshua in Hebrew; and the Greek form of Joshua is——what?"

"*Jesus*!" said Hiram, "Oh, it's not irreverent! Jesus and Saviour mean the same thing! I'm very glad."

"Are you satisfied, young McRoss?"

"Yes indeed, Mr. Grant. Oh, I'm so sorry you're going away."

"It is only for a week; and Mr. Slow is not at all afraid to take charge. Ronald has good-naturedly offered to help him, if necessary; and his salary will be doubled during my absence. *I* am sorry to leave you, my dear boy; but, don't forget, young McRoss, that *the same God* watches over us both?"

CHAPTER XVI.

"THAT BLESSED BOY."

N Wednesday morning Mr. Grant took his departure. The assistant felt quite unwell, but did not complain. Towards noon, however, he was obliged to take to his bed and send for Dr. Mays, who did not attempt to conceal his alarm, when he observed the symptoms. After some time, the physician came downstairs; and going to the school-room, summoned Ronald. A number of lads also approached.

"McFarlane," said the doctor, seriously, "this is a bad case. I fear I can do nothing. You must take all the responsibility of teaching, upon yourself; for I fear that Mr. Slow will never enter this room again. It is a very bad case of typhus fever, malignant and infectious. I hope it will not spread in the Seminary. Happily, Giovanni is visiting me; I shall not tell him his uncle is sick, for Mr. Slow does not wish it. The poor lad has no constitution and could not stand a severe attack, which he would be sure to have, for it would be impossible to keep him from his uncle's room, if he knew of his illness. *I* shall keep him and put him through a course of Chemistry so that he will not be losing his time. I am coming again in about an hour with medicines."

So he did—and, after seeing Mr. Slow, called Ronald aside privately, and charged him to allow none of the scholars to enter the sick room; above all, to keep away from it himself, or the disease would spread in the Seminary and the boys die off like rotten sheep.

"There is no danger of us going near him, poor man!" said McFarlane, gravely. "Our lives are valuable to us. It is quite unnecessary to charge the boys to avoid going in to see Mr. Slow, for they are very much afraid. George Thorne and a few others are in terror lest they contract the disease and die. They actually begged me to let them go home; but that I refused to do in the absence of the Principal. Doctor, I shall not charge them, nor say more about it than I can help; for you see it would never do to have a panic in the school."

"Of course not. Use your own judgment. Those who are so terrified are all the more liable to take the fever. Are *you* afraid yourself?" he asked abruptly.

Ronald never spoke anything but the truth. His black eyes looked full into those of the physician, as he candidly replied, "I *am* a little afraid of the typhus fever, doctor; you see *I am not ready to die!*"

"My young friend, you should *get* ready!" seriously answered the physician, and he departed.

In the meantime the boys were gathered in knots about

the school-room. The excitement amounted almost to a panic as Ronald had said.

"Archie Campbell, you keep very calm," observed Tom, in a trembling voice. "Aren't you at all afraid?"

"Not of dying," said Archie, earnestly, " but we would none of us like to have a fatal illness, away from all our friends. They will not send for our parents if we *do* take sick, for the disease is so contagious. Of course I am willing to die, if God see fit; but Tom, I would like to see my mother once more!" and the tears came into Archie's blue eyes.

"So would I," said Harding huskily, and turned away his head.

Ronald came in at this juncture, and rang the bell for school. The boys were only kept in for an hour, however, because it was late when they were called together. Poor Mr. Slow lay in bed, dreadfully frightened, for the doctor had been very plain with him. Suddenly he heard voices outside his door. Hiram McRoss was begging John to let him in, and make no fuss about it; he said that Ronald had not given any orders and he *must* see the assistant. John was greatly surprised but allowed him to go, knowing he was Mr. Grant's favourite, and went all over the house whenever he pleased. Mr. Slow was dangerously ill—would probably never get better—and there was no one to speak a word of Christ, who alone could save his lost soul. *That* was enough for Hiram. The lad was well acquainted with his companions' fears; but he felt none himself. Baby he might be, as far as Mr. Grant was concerned, but Hiram McRoss was no coward. He boldly entered the sick room and sat down close to the assistant.

"Oh dear!" said our poor old, snarly friend, "you ought not to come in here! What will the Principal say if you get sick and die? The doctor says *I'm* not likely to recover, but that is no reason why *you* should risk your life."

"Do not trouble yourself about *me*, sir; I'm not at all afraid. Mr. Slow," he went on, tenderly, "don't you want a Friend—a Saviour, even Jesus, in your hour of need?"

"I *do;* but Hiram, I've spurned him in health, and He will not listen to me now!"

"Have you tried Him, sir?"

"No; it's useless. I know I'm a sinner—have known it all along; is it likely that, after rejecting Christ for years, He will receive me now?"

"Indeed, He will, sir. He is waiting with open arms! Won't you trust yourself to Him? Then He will save you and make you happy, both here and in heaven. Do not hesitate, please. Oh, Mr. Slow, *you can have instant salvation, by this instant committing your soul to Christ.*"

"Are you *sure* of that?"

"*Certain.*"

"Well," said the poor, weary assistant, "I will," and he closed his eyes. Opening them again, he asked: "Hiram, pray for me, that's a good boy."

Young McRoss knelt down; though he could not conduct family worship, he could pray for a dying sinner.

When he arose, Mr. Slow grasped his hand, exclaiming: " I'm happier than ever I was in my life ! Oh, what a fool I have been to keep the Blessed Saviour from my heart for so long. How patiently He waited—year after year —and I would not admit Him; but *He has come in now*," and the face of the assistant shone.

The tears ran down Hiram's cheeks; he could not say a word.

" Don't cry," said Mr. Slow, " I have treated you very badly, but I am so glad you forgave me, and risked your life that I might be saved."

Hiram brushed away his tears. " *You* have far more to forgive *me*, sir," he said, in a broken voice, " for I have been a most troublesome scholar, both to yourself and the Principal."

" Read a chapter for me, Hiram, please; something about Christ."

The lad did so, Mr. Slow listening with an expression of great content. A hymn or two followed; not sang, but repeated in a low, gentle voice, and Hiram arose to go.

Mr. Slow clasped his hand again, tightly, saying: " Good bye, God bless you, my dear boy. I don't wonder that Mr. Grant is so fond of you."

With tears in his eyes, McRoss passed out into the hall. He went immediately to the spacious garden, away from the other lads, and walked about for an hour, until tea was ready. He hoped that the fresh air would take all infectious matter from his clothes; for, though fearless as regarded himself, he did not wish to convey the contagion to his frightened companions, who had no idea where he had been. However, the first thing on entering the gárden, before he commenced his tramp, Hiram went into a lovely little harbour, and, kneeling down, gave most earnest thanks to God for converting the assistant.

On visiting his patient, the next morning the doctor was surprised to find him so calm and happy, in spite of the fact that there was very little hope of his recovery. After the school closed for the day, Hiram hastened upstairs.

"I'll not object to your going in," said John, "for whatever is to be gotten from the man, you have gotten it already."

"I'm not afraid," was the quiet answer, and Mr. Slow's face brightened at the sight of his young visitor.

"This is very kind, Hiram. Now read something more about Jesus. I have been thinking of Him all the day."

The lad immediately complied, by reading a chapter or two, and then the assistant called for some hymns. "Jesus lover of my soul," "Rock of Ages," "Just as I am," and "I lay my sins on Jesus," were reverently repeated by Hiram, and the sweet words at length soothed the weary Mr. Slow to sleep. McRoss immediately went off by himself into the garden.

The next morning the physician announced that his patient was quite delirious, and there was no hope of his recovery. The excitement of the boys became fearful.

"Oh, Dr. Mays," said Ronald, "is it too late to send for the Principal?"

"I telegraphed for him at the first, because I felt sure of a fatal result. He ought to be home to-day."

"Indeed, I'm very glad; it is impossible for me to quiet the alarm of those boys. Won't you come again this afternoon, sir?"

"If you wish it, McFarlane; but it seems useless."

When school was over, Hiram at once sought the bed-side of his sick teacher. He was still delirious, but recognised the lad, and asked for some hymns, which apparently soothed him for he closed his eyes.

There were smothered voices in the hall; suddenly the door opened, and Mr. Grant and the physician entered. They were startled by the sight of Hiram, sitting on the bed-side, close to the assistant, who had one of the lad's hands in his own.

For a moment the medical man was speechless; then he said, angrily: "I advise the Principal to get a cowhide and flog that young fellow until his back is raw; I'm sure he deserves it."

The half-conscious assistant paid no attention, and the doctor went on, in a louder tone, "*You're a bad boy, Hiram McRoss.*"

The name, coupled with the words that he had so often applied to the lad himself, aroused Mr. Slow. He opened his eyes and, looking wildly around, demanded: "Who says that Hiram McRoss is a bad boy? He is *not*. I was altogether mistaken, and wronged him much. I should have died in my sins had it not been for *him*! But he led me to the Saviour—*my* Saviour now. Afraid to die! Oh, no—not the least afraid; I lean entirely on Jesus. Hiram McRoss bad! No; no! Never you speak a word against *that blessed boy* again!" The voice of the assistant died away in incoherent murmurs.

"Sir," said John (who had come into the room soon after Hiram did), in a respectful tone, to the Principal, " Mr. Slow did not expect to live long enough to see you, and left me a message to deliver when you came back. This is it. "Tell Mr. Grant that his young McRoss has taught me the way to Christ and heaven!"

The master's heart was full, he could not reply, but hastily left the room. Hiram gently withdrew his hand, as Mr. Slow was evidently unconscious, and went out into the garden. Half an hour later the door of the Principal's sleeping apartment opened, and that gentleman came out. John noticed that his eyes were red. He inquired in a low voice, "Where is young McRoss?"

"Out in the garden, sir—he was longing to go into your room, I know, but was afraid of taking infection."

Hiram was pacing to and fro among the shady walks, when suddenly he came upon the Principal. There was a moment of bewilderment, and then young McRoss was locked in the master's arms. For some time neither of them spoke.

"Are *you* vexed with me, sir?" at length inquired Hiram, who was a baby again now, and crying on Mr. Grant's breast.

"Oh no, my darling, you have done *well*, you have done *bravely.*"

"The doctor thought it was wrong, but, indeed, I meant to do right."

"I know it, my boy, and am very glad that you have been such a blessing to my poor assistant."

The Principal did not think it necessary to send the lads home—and in a few days' time the doctor, to his own great astonishment, began to entertain hopes of his patient's recovery. The crisis passed, Mr. Slow did not sink and die, as the physician expected.

"My dear sir, it must be your good spirits that keep you up," said the medical man one day.

The assistant smiled. "I would like to get well," he answered, "and live the rest of my life to the glory of Him who loved me and gave Himself for me."

And he *did* get well, though it was some time before he was strong enough to teach all his classes, which were taken up by degrees.

Hiram had a touch of the fever, but very slight. John, on the contrary, had it badly, while two of the maid servants, who washed the infected clothes, took it in its most severe form. One of them died, and the doctor had a hard task to save the other. To the relief of Thorne, it did not spread among the lads.

Mr. Slow took his place in the school-room a changed man. He had actually been at warfare with his own conscience for years. It was *that* that had made him so peevish and snarly. Now everything looked bright. He had a dear Friend, even Christ, ever by his side, and a glorious Home in prospect. There was no longer any temptation to snarl. The lads grew right fond of him; but, as was only natural, he loved Hiram, that "blessed boy," as he called him, above all the rest.

When Giovanni came home he was a little indignant at being kept in the dark concerning the illness of his uncle; however, the assistant soon convinced him that it was for the best. Before Giovanni had been in the house an hour he sought out Will Manning and asked if he had received a letter from Rosa Wright.

"Oh, yes," said the young man, "actually, Somerville, you think of nothing else but Temperance. What a lot of work for the cause you will get through in a lifetime if you go on as you have begun, Are you bound by oath to do it?"

Giovanni gravely bowed his head.

Manning looked surprised. "Well, I wouldn't take a pledge like *that*," he said, "but I'll sign the usual one against liquor. Rosa has no objection, she wishes me to write her name under my own."

"Good for Miss Rosa!" exclaimed Giovanni, joyfully, "I take back what I said—I *wouldn't* like to box her ears."

CHAPTER XVII.

CONFISCATED LIQUOR.

ONE night, after Mr. Slow had commenced to do a little in the school-room, the Principal was sitting by Hiram's bedside, when there was a knock at the door. Mr. Grant opened it and admitted Ronald McFarlane.

"Excuse me, sir, please. Ivon is crying with toothache—will you allow me to go into his room and put some aquafortis in the tooth?"

"Certainly, you are welcome to relieve him if you can."

"Thank you, sir," and McFarlane departed.

The weeping child was surprised by his entrance with a lamp, a small phial, and something in a glass. After soaking a bit of cotton-wool in the strong liquid, he carefully stuffed it into the aching tooth, and, when poor Ivon was a little quieted, he took the glass and said, "Drink this, my dear, and you will soon be fast asleep." Ivon did so unquestioningly; and Ronald went back to his room, where he prepared a big tumbler-full for himself of the *same* kind of drink that he had given the child.

The following morning at breakfast, Ivon warmly praised McFarlane for his kindness.

"What did you put in the tooth?" inquired Mr. Slow, "oil of smoke?"

"No, sir, it was nitric acid," replied Ronald.

"You said aquafortis last night," remarked Hiram.

Mr. Grant smiled. "I must teach you a little chemistry some of these days, young McRoss. Nitric acid and aquafortis are one and the same thing."

Hiram laughed and looked slightly confused.

"Ivon," suddenly exclaimed Ronald, "you must take the pledge again. That was *brandy* that I gave you last night to set you to sleep. Don't look so horrified, child— it's not *your* fault."

Ivon began to cry. "I never tasted a drop of the stuff in my life before. Oh, it's too bad, Ronald."

"So it is. I'm very sorry I was so thoughtless. It was one of Mr. Gordon's remedies."

"McFarlane," asked the Principal, "do you keep a little bottle of brandy by you in case of tooth-ache?"

"No, sir," replied Ronald, who would not even try evasion to clear himself. "I keep the brandy in large bottles, and not for tooth-ache, but to drink."

For a moment Mr. Grant and his assistant were speechless at the bold confession, then the former seriously inquired, "How much liquor have you, McFarlane?"

"About three bottles of rum and two and a half of brandy."

"When do you drink it?"

"Every night, sir—except when you were away—I did not taste it then."

"How did you get the liquor—when I was absent?"

"Oh, no, Mr. Grant, I did not get any *then.* It was very wrong, but I bribed one of the servants. Please do not ask who it was, for it would be dishonourable in me to inform, as it was entirely my own fault."

"I must insist on your telling me if it were John, whom I have always considered faithful."

"No, sir, it was *not* John—neither was it that poor girl who died."

"I will not question you further on that point," said the master, sternly. "I might have *known* it was a woman."

The lads laughed, but were checked by a grave look from the Principal, who continued—" It seems needless to ask—of course, McFarlane, you have not been intoxicated since coming here?"

The young man's face burned as he answered, "Yes, I have, Mr. Grant—*that* was the cause of all those headaches."

"Ronald," exclaimed George Thorne, "I don't believe you would tell a lie, even to save your life."

"I should hope not," earnestly returned McFarlane.

"Did not you know you were breaking the rules?" asked the master.

"Yes, sir, I broke them wilfully, and cannot expect you to have any mercy on me."

"Are you fond of liquor?" asked the Principal, not at all unkindly.

"Yes, sir, *very.* I *love* that detestable rum-bottle and *hate* it too."

Mr. Slow could keep silence no longer. " He is too fine a fellow for you to cast off, my superior. Keep him here by all means, but make him give up his liquor to you and destroy it."

"That will be the best thing, Mr. Slow, certainly it will," said the master. "I rely on your honour, McFarlane, to bring me every drop you have; and, remember, you must promise to bribe that woman (whoever she is) no more."

"I promise, Mr. Grant," answered Ronald, gratefully, "and I will hand what I have over to you, immediately after breakfast. You are very good not to expel me in disgrace," and a mist came over McFarlane's black eyes, so that he could scarcely see the Principal and his companions. Mr. Slow noticed it, and at once took the attention of the lads from Ronald by proposing a picnic which delighted them much.

The three bottles of rum, two and a half of brandy, and a flask of alcohol, were given up to the Principal, who asked, " Don't you want this alcohol, Ronald, for chemical purposes ?"

"That is what I bought it for, Mr. Grant."

" You could not drink *this* ?"

"I *have* drunk it, sir, diluted with water and sweetened when I was out of other liquors."

" Poor boy !" said Mr. Slow, who was standing by his superior's side.

The housekeeper entered the room at this moment, and seeing what was going on, hurriedly came forward. Laying her hand on Ronald's shoulder, she exclaimed, " Oh, I'm very glad. Often have I blamed myself for affording you the means of temptation, and will do so no more."

" Was it *you* ? " inquired the astonished Principal, in a tone of disgust, for he had not suspected his housekeeper —" *all women are alike!* "

" Yes, *I* got it for him—the bonnie laddie ! " said the worthy Mrs. Brown.

" It was all my fault. *You* are not to blame," returned Ronald.

" I differ from you," said the Principal. " Now, McFarlane, carry that liquor out doors and pour every drop of it in the dust."

It is needless to add that Mr. Grant saw the command fully executed. McFarlane faithfully kept his promise, and did not attempt to obtain intoxicating liquor by bribery or any other way. He would not sign the pledge, for he declared that if temptation came in his way it would be impossible to resist it. In vain Giovanni pleaded with him concerning Almighty strength ; Ronald McFarlane obstinately refused to " bind his soul by a vow."

Dr. Mays had organized a Band of Hope in Roseville, to which Giovanni belonged, though he could not attend very regularly.

The day of the picnic arrived. It was clear and bright, but very warm. The students were to play a game of cricket with the village lads, and a good time was expected. The picnic was held in a beautiful grove belonging to Mr. Grant. To the delight of the seminary boys they beat their opponents from Roseville, but there was great good-nature over the result. Ronald and Hiram distinguished themselves, but Will Manning outdid them both, greatly to the amazement of his comrades. Mr. Slow stood near, looking on, while on a knoll a short distance off, Mr. Grant was sitting under a shady tree Now and then he would raise his eyes from the book he was reading to see how the game was progressing. At last it was over. While the rest laughed and talked over the result Hiram hastened to the knoll, and tired, hot, hatless and coatless, threw himself at full length on the ground beside the master. Then creeping a little closer he laid his head on Mr. Grant's lap. That gentleman's book dropped unheeded by his side, and he petted Hiram to his heart's content.

In the meantime an enterprising photographer, who had lately arrived in the village, began to take pictures of the various groups. In one he had the Band of Hope boys and girls from Roseville, Giovanni among them. They all wore their badges, and looked well. As they were taking their places Giovanni found Hattie Mays by his side, and immediately took her hand in his, which caused the artist to smile. Another group consisted of the assistant-teacher and the students from Roseville seminary. Hiram McRoss was not among them; he was half asleep on Mr. Grant's knee.

"Who is that fine-looking gentleman over there under the tree?" asked the artist.

"That is the Principal of our Seminary," answered Mr. Slow.

"Oh, I'll go and ask him if he has any objection to being taken."

He did immediately. The master gravely assented. McRoss roused himself, but did not attempt to get up.

"And who are you, my lad?" asked the artist.

"I'm Mr. Grant's baby," said Hiram McRoss.

The photographer laughed, and went to place his instrument in position. The picture was very life-like, and pleased the Principal so much that he ordered several of them.

"Who is that lad lying under the tree near the headmaster?" asked the artist of Aleck, "he would not tell me his name, but only said he was Mr. Grant's baby."

Shuter laughed. "He spoke the truth! His name is Hiram McRoss."

"The Principal seems very fond of him. I am sure he ordered the pictures because Hiram looked so extremely natural. As for Mr. Grant, anybody would know it for him half a mile off. Now I'm going to take one of that boy and girl who stood so lovingly hand-in-hand."

"Giovanni Somerville and Hattie Mays!" said Shuter, "*I* saw them. That will be a match just as sure as anything."

"Perhaps so," laughed the man, and he went to look up the "boy and girl."

It was some time before he could discover them. At last he caught sight of a little couple, wandering about together, and immediately gave pursuit. He came suddenly upon them, but the conversation was not of "love," as he expected. It was about the Temperance Cause. To the artist's great amazement Giovanni and Hattie set upon him at once to sign the Pledge. He might perchance have refused the boy, but the pleading, blue eyes of the girl were too much for him, so he gave them his name. They willingly consented to stand for another picture, and were taken as before, only much larger. When Dr. Mays saw the negative, he declared it was first rate, and ordered a dozen photographs to be printed from it.

Meanwhile, Ronald McFarlane was roaming around in search of ferns and other botanical specimens, of which he carried home an enormous bunch. He no longer made any secret of the darling wish of his heart, which was *to be a philosopher!*

The day was a very happy one for all concerned.

"What are you thinking of, Hiram?" asked Ronald, one fine afternoon.

"Of those clouds, McFarlane."

"So was I. Tell me your thoughts."

"Tell me *yours.*"

"Very well; I was merely thinking of the classes which those clouds belonged to."

"I don't understand."

Ronald took out his pocket-book and drew sketches of the different classes of clouds—cumulus, cirrus, stratus—and their combinations, cirro-cumulus, cirro-stratus, and cumulo-stratus. He then drew a picture of a nimbus or rain-cloud. It was all new to McRoss, who listened in surpise.

"Now tell me *your* thoughts," said McFarlane.

Hiram coloured. " Perhaps you will think me silly, Ronald, but those magnificent masses of heaped-up clouds (which you call cumuli) remind me of the clouds of glory in which Jesus will come."

."Would you be glad to see Him ? " abruptly inquired Ronald.

" Oh yes, *so* glad," said Hiram, and his face brightened at the thought.

" *I* shouldn't," gravely returned McFarlane, as he walked away.

A week passed. " Mr. Grant will be sure to march us into the dining-room after supper, to study that detestable algebra, which none of us could master save Ronald," said Shuter to his companions.

His surmises proved correct. The culprits were duly walked in, and seated at the long table.

" Can't you do it, young McRoss ? " asked the Principal kindly. " Let me help you."

" I've tried it half-a-dozen times already, sir, and I won't attempt it again."

" You must."

Hiram did not answer, but angrily flung the book across the table, over Thorne's head, upon the floor.

"I'll make you try that problem again," said the Principal gravely, " but not just yet. I shall flog you, young McRoss, as soon as you are over your fit of passion."

" I'm over it now, Mr. Grant," replied Hiram calmly.

" Very well—come with me into the school-room," and the two went out together.

" He has locked the door," observed Thorne, uneasily, who had slyly followed them, and then returned to his companions.

" Young McRoss," said the master, " you will have to use your hands afterwards, so I must ask you to take off your coat."

Hiram did so, and began to unbutton his vest. Like many of the other scholars, he wore a linen suit; so Mr. Grant said, " you need not take off your vest, my boy. I can hurt you enough without, for you are thinly dressed.' He then commenced the punishment, which was a very severe one—far too much so, though the Principal did not suspect it at the time. Hiram did not cry or complain, though the severity of the chastisement made him feel sick and weak.

The lads who were studying heard the sound of the strokes and soon Mr. Slow looked anxious—Ronald McFarlane also. " It's a shame," said Will Manning, as he knitted his brows. Thorne waited to hear no more, but put his hands over his ears. At last, Tom pushed him, saying, " They're coming back." Mr. Slow never raised his eyes, but the others did. Hiram came first, looking very pale. He sat down and opened the Algebra, which Archie had picked up and placed ready for him. The Principal stood close beside him.

"Mr. Grant, you're not going to stand," said Hiram half rising from his seat.

"Sit still, young McRoss," replied the master, " I prefer to stand."

The lad commenced to put down the problem. As the book would not stay open on the table, the Principal laid his hand upon it. In looking over the book, Hiram bowed his head and kissed the master's hand. Some of the boys laughed, but the Principal did not. He would have returned it, but was afraid of making Hiram cry. So he only asked very gently, " Was that kiss for whipping you, young McRoss ? "

" Yes, sir."

Mr. Slow looked keenly at Hiram. " You have flogged that boy far too hard, my superior," he gravely observed, " See how pale he is."

Strangely enough, the master had not noticed it. He did now and felt alarmed.

" Do you feel sick, my darling ? " asked the Principal anxiously.

"Yes, sir," and Hiram leaned his head against the master.

" Ivon, get him some cold water," said Mr. Slow ; and the child hastened to obey.

The Principal, who bitterly blamed himself for his severity, threw some of the water over the head and face of his favourite.

Hiram smiled. " I'm not going to faint, Mr. Grant ; I never fainted in my life ; it was only a strange, sick feeling."

George Thorne's eyes were flaming and all the lads felt indignant but were afraid to speak out. To their astonishment, Will Manning gravely observed, "The punishment was far too severe for a momentary fit of passion."

"So it was," said the assistant. "Why did you not tell him so, at the time, McRoss? He would not have whipped you any more, then."

"Mr. Grant knew best, sir," replied Hiram.

The Principal answered, in a low voice and quite huskily, "I'm afraid, young McRoss, that, in this case, Mr. Grant *didn't* know best." So saying, he took Hiram upstairs. Instead of letting him go to his own little room however, the master led him into *his*, put him to bed bathed his shoulders with warm water and applied soothing ointment to relieve the pain. The Principal was greatly shocked to find how badly he had cut his muchloved young McRoss.

Hiram was too much delighted at the thought of sleeping with Mr. Grant, to be anything else than wakesome, aside from the pain of the flogging. He wriggled and twisted about until past one o'clock. Finally, he went to sleep, after creeping as close to the Principal as it was possible to get. That gentleman was afraid to stir.

Hiram's cheek was pressed close to the master's bosom; the master's arms were around him. Partly from exhaustion—partly from the happy frame of mind, in which he sank off into dreamland—Hiram slept soundly. When he awoke the next morning, it was to find the Principal, dressed in his usual black broad-cloth suit, standing over him, inquiring how he had rested.

"I rested *well*, sir," replied the lad, "but am so sorry that I didn't awake first;" and he began to twist about uneasily.

"Do you feel very sore and stiff?" asked the Principal, sadly.

"Yes, sir; but I deserve *that*; it will do me good. Oh, I fully intended to awake before you."

"*Why*, young McRoss?"

No answer.

The master was surprised. "I would like to know. What—tears in your eyes, child. Are you so much disappointed as that?"

Hiram brushed them away. "I may not have another chance, and am *so* sorry. You will only be vexed if I tell you. Don't ask me, please—you would never let me."

"Let you do what?" inquired the head-teacher, who was thoroughly puzzled. "Young McRoss, you do not generally keep things from *me*."

"Oh! Mr. Grant, don't be vexed, please. Of course, if you were asleep you would not have known it. *I wanted to kiss you.*"

For a moment the Principal could not speak. His eyes were as full of tears as Hiram's. The boy asked in a low voice, "Are you angry with me, sir?"

"Oh, no, my darling!" said the master, huskily.

After wiping the tears from his eyes, the dignified head-teacher bent down over Hiram, saying, gently, "Young McRoss, you may kiss me now if you choose."

Hiram put his arms around Mr. Grant's neck, and, with

a mixture of love and reverence, pressed his lips to the master's cheek. Then, releasing the Principal, he said, very gratefully, "Thank you, dear Mr. Grant. So often I have wished to kiss you, but never dared."

"My little pet, I'm glad I have found it out. Do not be afraid of me for the future. I am *your father*, young McRoss."

Hiram was not well enough to come into the schoolroom that day, but he lay on a lounge in the parlour. When the hours of study were over, he sat in an easy-chair under a big elm tree, watching the sports he could not join. Some of the lads gathered around him, and expressed their sympathy. He immediately told them that he did not deserve any.

"Hiram," suddenly inquired Archie, "what if Mr. Grant got real angry with you some day, and did not like you any more?"

"I hope that will *never* be."

"Well—just suppose it."

"Of course," replied Hiram, sadly, "my earthly life would be shadowed all through; but *One*, dearer even than the Principal, would be with me in the shade as He has been in the sunshine. And," added the boy, his lips quivering, "in Heaven, Mr. Grant would love me again.'

"Supposing, though, that you lost Christ too?"

Hiram smiled. "Mr. Grant says that I *can't* lose *Him!*"

"The Principal evidently believes in the final perseverance of the saints," said Archie.

* N

"But what if a Christian sin and go astray," asked Thorne.

Hiram gravely answered, "Mr. Grant says that if we go astray God will scourge us until we return to Him."

"Does he know that by experience?" dryly inquired Archie.

Hiram's face reddened. "No, I don't think so," he answered, warmly. "I don't believe that Mr. Grant *could* go far astray. He lives too close to the Saviour for that. *I* know him better than any of you do."

"Well," said Thorne, "but suppose a Christian should sin grievously (not by sudden temptation, the best might fall in that way, and quickly get up again, but wilfully), and continues obstinately to sin, perhaps for weeks or months."

"Then," earnestly replied Hiram, "he might expect to have his whole life blighted."

"Would God do *that*?" asked Thorne, in dismay.

"Doubtless He would—in mercy to the man's soul. The wicked *may* perchance sin without feeling His hand in *this life*, but his own children never! Their chastisement is a sure thing, and if necessary it will be severe enough to blast their happiness for years—or all their earthly lives."

"Oh, dear!" said George Thorne, "then if ever I become a Christian I will try to walk straight."

"You will be very sorry if you sin," said Hiram, gently, "but not so much for the chastisement."

"What then?"

McRoss replied, in a low voice, "You will be more sorry that you have grieved your Lord than for any correction that He may please to give you."

Tom Harding had listened to the whole conversation in silence ; he now gravely observed, " There is no danger that Hiram will lose the love of Mr. Grant, for friends in Jesus are friends for ever." So saying, he left the group, and joined the rest of his companions at play.

In going to bed that night, Thorne inquired, "Tom, what ails you ? You never tease Hiram now, and act so queerly. You are twice as long in saying your prayers as you used to be; that Bible does not lie unopened from one Sabbath to another, but the marker moves on every day. I don't *see* you read the Book, but it never gets dusty like mine. What is the matter with you ? "

Tom answered gravely, "we were all afraid when the assistant was so ill. I waited until that Temperance boy came home, and——"

" Go on," said Thorne.

Tom replied in a low voice, " George, if I ever get to Heaven, I shall be a star in the crown of Giovanni Somerville ! "

CHAPTER XVIII.

THE TEMPERANCE BANNER.

TWO weeks before the mid-summer vacation, there was to be a Temperance celebration in Roseville, Giovanni was eager to attend, and coaxed Ronald to go too. Thorne also begged permission to accompany them, which the master granted, and the three set off, one fine morning, for the village.

"How clear that water is!" observed George, as he halted at a bridge over a small stream, some quarter of a mile from the Seminary.

"Beautifully clear," replied Ronald. "What is the programme for the day?" he continued, as they moved on.

"A procession at eleven o'clock; and then dinner in the hall; after which there will be Temperance speeches, songs etc."

"Well, my young friend, *you* will have to walk in that procession, so I advise you not to hurry along so, now. There is plenty of time. The day is very warm and you will be tired out before it is over."

Giovanni smiled and slackened his pace.

The procession was worth looking at—so Thorne thought —and the dinner excellent. After it was over, the speeches commenced, interspersed with songs and dialogues. Ronald had unfortunately got seated with some young rowdies from Roseville, who had come to ridicule the whole thing. The allusions they made to wine, etc., aroused the appetite of McFarlane, which was all the more fierce for his temporary abstinence. They judged, from their new companion's dress, that he had plenty of money; and proposed to adjourn to a tavern. Thorne saw them go out and felt anxious. Giovanni's attention was otherwise occupied.

While the speeches were going on, Dr. Mays was summoned away. He first publicly presented Giovanni with a beautiful Temperance Banner, to hang in his room, which greatly pleased our young friend. Then, taking his daughter with him, for it was her aunt that had been suddenly taken ill, the physician drove off in his double-seated carriage, promising to be back, if possible, before the meeting closed. However, he did not come; and Giovanni and Thorne started for home. Passing a tavern, Ronald came out quite intoxicated—his three companions also. They were going to see McFarlane part of the way home, they said. They had none of them taken enough to be incapacitated by the liquor, just the reverse.

George Thorne was very much afraid, but hoped that the three young men, drunk though they were, would be some protection against Ronald. . Giovanni was dreadfully shocked; but not at all afraid.

Soon they left the village and turned up the road, leading to the Seminary. How Thorne wished that the mile was over, and they were safely there. The three rowdies laughed, danced and sang—while Ronald cursed and swore;

not at *them*, but his Temperance companions. He abused Thorne for taking the Pledge until poor George was half beside himself with fear.

At last they came to the bridge. Ronald suddenly stopped and telling his three drunken comrades that *now* they would have some fun, he seized Giovanni and carried him down the slope to the edge of the stream. Then, with a fearful oath, he told young Somerville that he should break his Pledge or die.

" I will die," said Giovanni.

Ronald put the lad down, and there the rowdies laughingly closed around him to prevent his escape.

McFarlane took a small bottle of wine from his pocket, and told Giovanni to take a drink and save his life.

The boy firmly refused.

" I'll drown you if you don't!—ah! you think I won't do it; *by the cause that you love I will.* It only needs a few glasses of liquor to make a devil of me."

George Thorne turned very pale, he knew the truth of Ronald's last words. Coward that he was, he could not fly and leave his young companion in such hands; but the two were helpless against McFarlane alone, who was very strong—to say nothing of the three rowdies who cheered him on. Jack Hill, one of the young ruffians, proposed that they should pour a mouthful or two down the boy's throat.

" No—no," said Ronald, with another dreadful oath, " *that* would not be breaking his pledge, it must be *his own act.* He shall take hold of the bottle and drink some wine himself, or else have the pleasure of dying for the Cause."

"I choose the last," replied Giovanni.

McFarlane angrily seized him and held him under water until half suffocated, then drew him out to give him one more chance.

When the lad got breath to speak, he still refused, and kissed the Temperance Banner, which he had held firmly in his hand when he went under water.

"Ha! ha!" laughed Ronald, "I have it: Do you remember that poetry, boy, composed by you when only ten years old? *I* do:

> 'Let me carry thy Temperance Banner
> To the very gate of Heaven.'

Now, you shall have that prayer answered. Carry the Banner, if you will, to the very throne of God—have you any last message to leave? If so, tell it to Thorne."

"He means it," warned George, who trembled with fear.

"Then," said Giovanni, calmly, "tell uncle and Dr. Mays to *work for Temperance*: ask the doctor to kiss Miss Hattie good-bye for me, and charge her ever, *ever*, EVER to be faithful to our Cause."

"I'll do it, shake hands, Giovanni."

The lad did so.

"I give you one more chance, you had better save your life, a single mouthful will do it," said Ronald.

"*Not a drop, God being my Helper*," replied young Somerville.

"Then," said McFarlane, "you deserve to die; it's quite fair, I appeal to the boys."

"*And I,*" answered Giovanni, with a shout of triumph, "*appeal to Jehovah, the God of the Temperance Cause.*"

Ronald instantly seized him and held him again under water. The three rowdies laughed. Thorne stood paralyzed for some time, then he feared for his own safety and fled up the bank, and out upon the road. They scarcely noticed his flight. After running a few yards, he heard the sound of wheels, Dr. Mays was returning to Roseville.

"God be praised, my life is safe," thought Thorne, as he rushed on.

The physician drew up sharply beside him, for he saw that something was wrong.

"O, doctor, Ronald McFarlane got drunk, and he is drowning Giovanni," was all that Thorne could say.

Hattie turned frightfully pale, her father seized the whip and applied it with such force that the horses started on a gallop, soon they were at the bridge, throwing the lines to his daughter, the physician hastily got out and hurried down the bank. He was afraid that a cold water ducking on such a hot day would give Giovanni a serious illness, that Ronald intended anything further, never entered the worthy gentlemen's mind. Rage made the doctor strong; he pushed McFarlane aside and drew Giovanni out, to his horror he found that the boy had ceased to breathe. The poor physician turned deathly pale, saying, "He's gone."

Then in a moment, the doctor's eyes flamed with anger, and he turned fiercely on Ronald, " You villain, you murderer! To the gallows you shall go."

The dreadful words sobered McFarlane, instantly.

Looking at the three rowdies, the doctor went on: "Jack Hill, Charles Thorpe, Bill McKays, you wicked wretches—a life-long sojourn in the penitentiary awaits you."

Then, rising, he was going to carry the boy; but the sudden shock had exhausted him and he could not do it.

"Let *me* carry him, sir; you are not able," said Ronald, who was a human devil no longer but fully himself again.

The physician unwillingly allowed him to do so.

In climbing the bank with the drowned lad carried tenderly in his strong arms, Ronald McFarlane breathed his first real prayer. It was, "God be merciful to me a sinner." Long had he known the way of Salvation and refused to profit by it; but now in his agony of darkness and misery, thankfully, oh so thankfully, did Ronald cast himself with all his sins upon Jesus and was saved. When he went down that bank he was a child of the devil, he reached the top of it again a child of God.

Hattie was very pale; her face looked hard and stony; but when her father took his place beside her and Ronald lifted the drowned boy into the carriage, laying him on the doctor's knees with his head in her lap, she began to weep bitterly.

" Get in, McFarlane," said the physician, sternly, " I

shall not lose sight of *you*. The other lads can be arrested anytime; they are going home, I see."

"I do not wish to evade justice, sir;" replied Ronald calmly, and he got into the carriage, sitting on the back seat with Thorne.

As the doctor urged on the horses, McFarlane drew a flask of brandy from his pocket, saying, "did you pour out that wine, George?"

"*Yes*, when you were carrying Giovanni up the slope."

Ronald flung the flask away with all his force, breaking it into fragments. "God helping me I will *never* drink another drop," he said.

"Very well;" bitterly returned Thorne, " but your remorse comes too late to save Giovanni. All his bright schemes of Temperance work frustrated and himself cut off in his boyhood. Then his old uncle who has no relative in the world but that young lad; and poor Hattie, how you have blighted her life; I should think it would make you feel miserable to see her tears dropping on that dead boy's face. You have wrought all this misery and put your soul in peril for *a glass of rum.*"

Ronald replied in a low voice, "you cannot blame me, George, as I blame myself."

Thorne said no more, and soon they stopped at the Seminary. The horror and amazement of both teachers and scholars may be imagined. Mr. Slow, overwhelmed with sorrow, did not speak; but his look of reproach cut Ronald to the heart.

Giovanni was carried upstairs and laid on his own little

bed. The Temperance Banner was firmly clasped in his cold hand. The lads were sent down to the school-room where Thorne told them the whole story. He then went into the housekeeper's domains and delivered Giovanni's message to Miss Hattie.

In about twenty minutes' time, Mr. Slow came down stairs.

"Is there any hope, sir?" asked Hiram, eagerly.

The assistant shook his head. "They are doing all they can; but what use is it?"

"None!" replied Ronald sadly, "I *know* he is dead."

"Could you tell when he died?" asked the horror-struck lads.

"Yes."

"Then, why didn't you take him out?"

"Because I wanted to make sure work."

"Ronald," exclaimed the astounded assistant, "do you mean to say that you *intended* to kill him?"

"Yes, sir."

"Be careful, McFarlane;" warned George, "all you say will be apt to come out in evidence against you at the trial."

"There won't be any trial."

"Yes, there will;" angrily exclaimed Tom. "The doctor's testimony and Thorne's will establish the case beyond doubt."

"It will not be necessary to have a trial," calmly replied Ronald, "for I shall plead guilty."

Tears filled Mr. Slow's eyes and silence fell on the lads.

They well knew what the consequences of such an act would be.

"Oh, McFarlane," said Thorne, at length, "in such a case as this, it surely could not be wrong for you to make your escape."

"I shall wait until all hope is over," returned Ronald, "and then give myself up to the authorities at Roseville."

"Had you any spite against my poor nephew?" asked the assistant.

"Oh, no, sir! I liked him well. But, when intoxicated, I would not scruple to murder my own father, if he vexed me!"

The boys looked horrified, and with good reason.

Hiram went close and put his arm around the assistant.

"It is a good thing that *you* are spared to me still," said poor Mr. Slow.

"Giovanni may come to, yet," observed Hiram, hopefully.

"But, Ronald knows when he died!" urged Shuter.

"Nonsense—McFarlane knew when he became insensible and lost all outward signs of life. But, he *may* recover consciousness, after all."

"So I think," said Will Manning, "there has not been time enough, yet."

Mr. Slow looked somewhat comforted and left the room. In ten minutes or so, he returned, saying that his nephew was recovering. What a load was taken from the heart of McFarlane! It is impossible to express his gratitude to God. The boys were joyful over the good news.

"What were the first words that Giovanni said, on awaking?" asked Thorne.

"The Cause!" answered Mr. Slow, with a smile.

No one was allowed to see the lad that day, save the doctor and the two teachers. After being sure that all was going on right, the physician drove his daughter home. First, however, he went into the school-room and informed the boys that Giovanni would not hear of McFarlane and his three companions being arrested—he fully forgave them. Ronald hastily went out.

"I'm glad of that," said Thorne, "we do not want McFarlane to get into trouble."

That evening, the teachers held an earnest consultation in the parlour (Hiram McRoss being with them), as to whether Ronald should be turned away. The Principal felt doubtful—Mr. Slow thought it would be best, in case McFarlane should attempt anything of the kind again; for, "Hiram's turn might come next!"

Mr. Grant turned pale.

"Then," said young McRoss, bitterly, "I hope that Ronald will kill me outright, for I do not want to suffer all the agonies of dying, and then come to life again (so to speak) as poor Giovanni did!"

"If McFarlane stays, he shall not have a chance to do any mischief," said the Principal.

After some further consultation, it was finally agreed that the question should be left to Giovanni, who at once announced his wish that Ronald should remain at the

Seminary. The next morning he asked the doctor if he could see one of his companions, *only one!*

"Perhaps," was the doubtful answer, "but you are so weak, that it must be for a very few minutes. Which of the lads is it, that you are so anxious to converse with?"

"Ronald McFarlane—I must see him alone!"

"Alone! Oh, no!"

"Oh, *yes!*" said Giovanni, earnestly. "You need not blame him, for it was the vile liquor that made him act so, he would not harm a beetle if he were himself!"

"Very well," said the Principal, "you shall see him alone, but only for ten minutes. The doctor and I will remain in the hall. Call us if we are wanted."

"That is quite unnecessary, sir."

The lads were greatly surprised, that of all his schoolfellows, Giovanni wished to see McFarlane first. The young man eagerly ascended the stairs and was soon shut in with the boy he had so nearly murdered. What passed between the two, Thorne and his comrades often wondered, but never found out. They saw, however, that Ronald's name was on the Pledge-roll, ever after that day. *Why* it was blotted, they had no idea, for all knew that the young man could write beautifully. That it *was* McFarlane's writing there could be no doubt, but they more than once told him that the blurred signature *was anything but a credit to him!

By and by, Mr. Grant called "McFarlane, your time is up!"

The door opened at once, and Ronald came out, crying like a child, with his face buried in his hands. Hastily passing them, he locked himself up in his own room. The Principal and his companion went in to see if the sick lad were excited, Mr. Slow just after them.

"Oh, uncle—Dr. Mays—Ronald is a Christian!" joyfully exclaimed Giovanni.

"It looks like it, truly," said the doctor in a most unbelieving tone, "he had better shew his faith by his works, before he tries to impose upon us in that way."

"McFarlane would never impose upon any one," said Mr. Slow, "but are you sure he told you so, my nephew?'

"Yes, sir, and Ronald could not speak anything but the truth. I knew there was no hope for him, save in the help of God; and, accordingly, asked him, most earnestly to come to Jesus for salvation from *every* sin. He immediately replied that he *had*. Oh, I'm so glad! Ronald McFarlane is safe enough now, because he is trusting in Christ!"

"Indeed, I am glad to hear it," said the Principal.

"And so am I," eagerly joined in Mr. Slow.

Dr. Mays looked grave and incredulous. Soon he inquired, "what did you think of, my lad, when that fellow put you under water?"

"Of all of you, sir, and of the Cause."

"Were you sorry that there was no further chance of working for it?"

"Yes, sir, until I recollected that God knew best."

"Did you pray for anything, my boy?" asked the physician, his voice trembling a little, "if so—what?"

"For uncle, for you and Miss Hattie, Dr. Mays, and of course, most especially for the Temperance Cause."

"What is the last thing you remember, Giovanni?"

"When I was losing my senses, you mean, sir—Oh, the last thing I remember, was commending my soul to Christ."

The doctor's heart was too full to seek further information. He stayed with Giovanni for over an hour and then went down to the school-room, where he found Ronald and his fellow-students. Neither of the teachers were present. The medical man at once commenced to give McFarlane a lecture before all the boys. The delinquent made no attempt to defend himself—finally, the physician came to a dead stop, partly for want of breath —just after telling McFarlane that he was a vile wretch, and would have a black account to render.

"You have forgotten to mention one thing, sir," replied the young man, gravely.

"What is *that*?" growled the doctor.

"The blood of Jesus Christ can wash even murderers white," replied Ronald, "I have tried it and I *know*."

George Thorne was thunderstruck—Hiram joyfully seized McFarlane by the hands, and warmly congratulated him; the doctor stalked out of the room incredulous no longer.

"That lad is quite in earnest," he said to himself, "what

a strange light shone in his eyes when he spoke of that precious blood. Giovanni was right after all."

A day or two passed. The assistant brought his nephew down stairs; and the cordiality that evidently existed between the recovered boy and McFarlane, soon restored the popularity of the latter.

Thorne's conscience gave him no rest. His formerly wicked chum, Tom, had "entered in at the strait gate," and was circumspectly walking in the "narrow way." And now, the words, " Ronald McFarlane's a Christian— *Ronald McFarlane's a Christian !* " kept sounding in his ears continually.

" McRoss," said he, one day, " will you tell me about your conversion ? "

Poor Hiram—he did not wish to do so, thinking that his thoughtless companion only inquired for amusement. " Why do you want to know, Thorne ? " he asked sadly, " probably, you don't believe I ever *was* converted."

" McRoss, why will you talk so. *I* want to be a Christian. It's about time," he added bitterly, " for my wicked chum, Harding, and that murderous Ronald McFarlane have actually entered the kingdom of God before me. I want to have my sins forgiven; if any one can help me, *you* can; I like *you*, and don't care to speak to other people about this matter."

Hiram's heart beat quickly with joyous surprise, God had used him once as His messenger to Mr. Slow—was it possible He meant to again ?

" If *that* is why you wish to know, Thorne, I will tell
o

you, of course," replied McRoss, in a gentle tone. And he did so; concluding by giving him a warm invitation to the Saviour.

"Will you pray for me, Hiram—*now?*"

After a moment's hesitation, McRoss answered "Yes," and the two lads went upstairs together.

When the boys were at home again for the holidays, George Thorne told his mother various items of school news—the assistant's illness—the great change in that gentleman—thecricket-match—Ronald McFarlane's crime and the good results that flowed from it, etc. When he had finished, she inquired, "My dear George, why are you so fond of Hiram, above all the rest of your schoolfellows?"

The boy earnestly answered, "because, mother, I am a Christian, now, and it was Hiram McRoss who brought me to Jesus."

THE END.

www.ingramcontent.com/pod-product-compliance
Lightning Source LLC
Chambersburg PA
CBHW021825230426
43669CB00008B/864